Simple Sewing
with a French Twist

Translation copyright © 2007 by Marabout

Published in the United States by Potter Craft, an imprint of the
Crown Publishing Group, a division of Random House, Inc., New York.
www.clarksonpotter.com
www.pottercraft.com

Originally published in France as *De Filles En Aiguilles* by Marabout
(Hachette Livre), Paris, in 2006.

Copyright © 2006 by Marabout

POTTER CRAFT and CLARKSON N. POTTER are trademarks, and POTTER
and colophon are registered trademarks of Random House, Inc.

Library of Congress Cataloging-in-Publication Data is available

ISBN-10: 0-307-35182-3
ISBN-13: 978-0-307-35182-1

Printed in China

10 9 8 7 6 5 4 3 2 1

First American Edition

Céline Dupuy

Simple Sewing with a French Twist

Photography by Marie-Pierre Morel
Design: Emmanuelle Javelle and Stéphanie Huré
Graphics and drawings: Anne Bullat Piscaglia

POTTER
CRAFT

Contents

Getting started   7

First steps   37

The nesting instinct   61

Warm and cozy   85

Kitchen essentials   109

Beautiful bath   133

Romance   157

For the little lady of the house   181

Out on the patio   205

Appendices   229

Index of sewing projects   254

Address book   255

Acknowledgments   256

Before you start...

Whether you're a complete beginner or you already know something about sewing, this is the book for you!

In these pages are over fifty easy-to-make projects for home and wardrobe, all with a wonderful sense of French style. Learn how to make chic and ultra-simple to more complicated projects, and try a whole range of skills and techniques for sewing by hand and by machine. So, if you're ready to take the plunge, make a date with your sewing machine (if you don't have one, borrow your grandmother's or even pick one up second hand) and try out a few samples using some of those old pieces of fabric tucked away in your closet.

This book is a goldmine of information that gives you all the advice you need—basic sewing lessons, step-by-step instructions and diagrams, and patterns. Start with something really simple—the throws, pillows, or a customized chair cushion are all easy to make—before moving on to the sun hat or the sweet chemise. A word of advice from one who knows—as long as you are precise, patient, and persistent, everything will work out fine, that's a promise. And last but not least, the real secret of success is the desire to do something for yourself and to surprise yourself. Iron, fold, cut, and pin with a foot on the pedal and an eye on the needle. Now you're ready to get started. So, off you go and ... enjoy!

Céline Dupuy

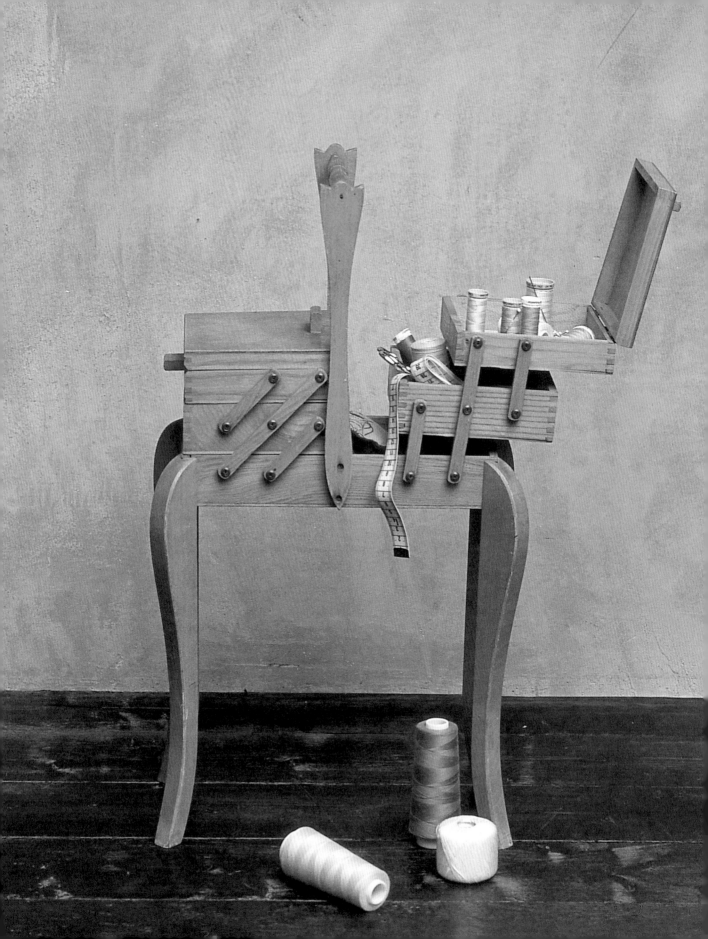

Getting started

(sewing box* and a few French sewing lessons)

* You'll need a box with compartments that's large enough to store your scissors, a few spools of thread, a tape measure, and needles. It's a good idea to store ribbon, embroidery thread, and other accessories in separate, clearly labeled boxes. That way you won't waste time searching for bits and pieces for those finishing touches.

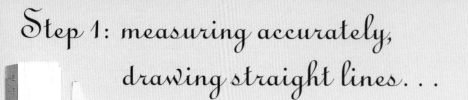

Step 1: measuring accurately, drawing straight lines...

Graduated rulers
12- and 36-inch rulers are useful for drawing straight lines.

Compasses
Compasses can come in handy for certain patterns, such as hats and round cushions.

Large set square
Ideal for drawing right angles directly onto fabric.

Tape measure
You'll need a 60-inch tape measure for measuring fabrics.

Handy hint...
Make sure you have a work surface large enough for the project you're making, so that the fabric can lay quite flat when you're drawing, cutting, and pinning.

Tailor's chalk
...or a fabric marking pencil is useful for drawing the outline of a pattern on fabric. But remember to cut ½ inch (1 cm) to the outside of the line—this is the seam allowance.

Ballpoint pen and pencil
These are ideal for drawing the outline of a pattern on materials such as oilcloth, leather, suede, and raffia.

Weights
Weights (paper weights or pebbles) are useful for keeping long lengths of fabric in place while you're drawing, pinning, and cutting.

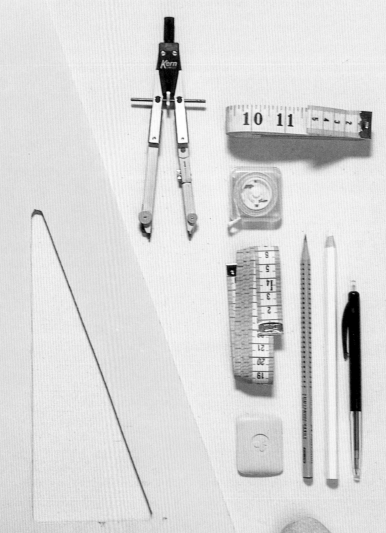

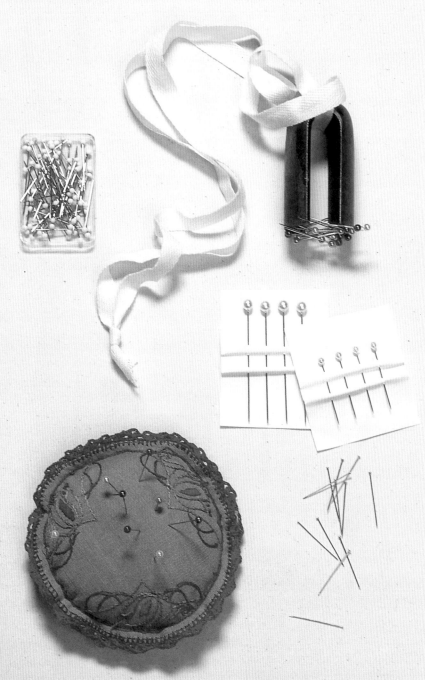

Magnet

A magnet is great for picking up those pesky little pins, especially when it's attached to a length of tape.

All-purpose pins

Buy a box of dressmaker's super-fine steel pins—they'll allow you to machine the fabric directly without having to baste. You simply insert the pins at right angles along the edge of the fabric at ¾-inch (2-cm) intervals.

Round-headed pins

Pins with round, colored heads are useful for marking particular points—e.g. quarter circles on hats, poufs, etc.—or for pinning thick fabrics or fur.

Pin cushion

A wrist pin cushion, as worn by the professionals, makes selecting your needles and pins much easier.

Cutting...

Scissors

Keep dressmaking scissors exclusively for sewing and, in particular, for cutting fabrics. That way you'll be sure they'll stay sharp enough to cut with the points as well as along the blades. It's best to buy a medium-sized pair of good-quality shears—keep a cheaper pair for cutting out patterns.

Pinking shears

Pinking shears have serrated blades for cutting zigzag edges that help keep fabric from fraying. They can be used to trim off excess fabric from the ½ inch (1 cm) seam allowance on curved seams.

Embroidery scissors

These are small, very pointed scissors used for precision cutting—trimming long threads, button holes, etc.

Seam ripper

A seam ripper is used for unpicking a badly sewn seam.

Tweezers

Tweezers are ideal for removing small pieces of thread from a seam unpicked with a seam ripper.

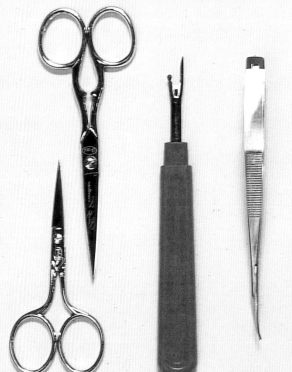

. . . and pressing

Whatever you're making, you'll need to go frequently from the sewing machine to the ironing board, and back again. . .

Remember. . .
Always press fabric before tracing the pattern onto it.

Always press a hem before sewing it.

Always press seams before pinning or basting a lining into place.

A word of advice
Make sure the temperature of the iron is adjusted to suit the type of fabric you're pressing.

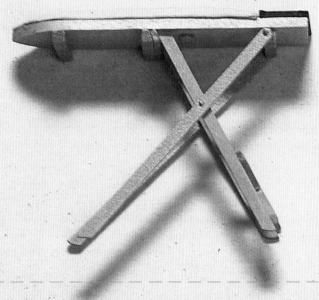

Needles and thread

Sewing machine needles

Choose a pack of assorted needles (they'll have different numbers) for fine and thicker fabrics. There are also special needles available that are designed for sewing leather.

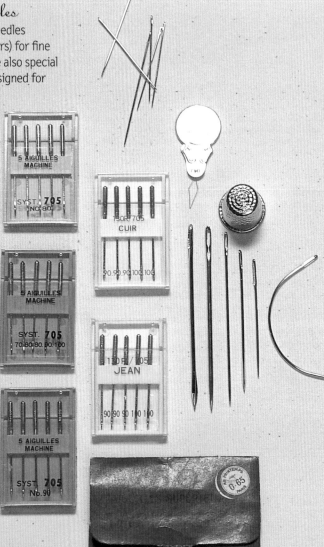

Metal thimble

A thimble is worn on the middle finger of your sewing hand, to protect it from needle pricks.

Needle threader

A threader makes it easier to thread a needle when your eyes are tired. Insert the metal loop through the eye of the needle, pass the thread through the metal loop, and pull the thread through the eye.

Sewing and embroidery needles

For sewing needles (pointed ends) and embroidery needles (rounded ends), choo packs of long needles in an assortment of sizes, from fine to sturdy. Sewing nee dles (sharps) are numbered according to thickness, from 1–10 (the finest).

Beading needles

Beading needles are long and very fine, and the threading hole is very narrow.

Leather needles

These needles have a beveled end to make sewing leather easier.

Upholstery and craft needles

These are often sold individually. Choose your needle according to what you want to use it for—e.g. threading a cord through a casing.

ways use a thread that matches
e fiber content of your fabric.

 a 100 percent cotton fabric,
 best to use a 100 percent
ton thread.

 a synthetic fabric, use a
thetic thread.

read comes on all kinds of
ferent spools, in a wide
iety of qualities, thicknesses,
terials, and quantities.
n't hesitate to ask for advice
ou're not sure.

Accessories

Polyester
fiberfill
(washable)

Binding and
iron-on bonding tape

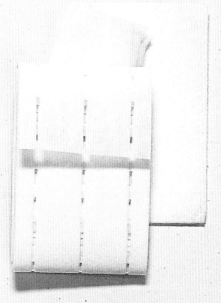

Polyester batting,
sold by the yard

There's a wide range of accessories to choose from—metal eyelets in various sizes, strips of eyelets for ready-to-hang drapes, metal clips for attaching sheer drapes to a slender pole, small lead weights sold by the yard for weighting the bottom of sheer drapes, safety pins for threading ribbon (or cord) through a casing, fusible stabilizers to reinforce a fabric, polyester fiberfill for stuffing cushions, batting for lining quilts and throws, zippers, self-cover buttons, decorative buttons, ribbons, cords... The list is endless.

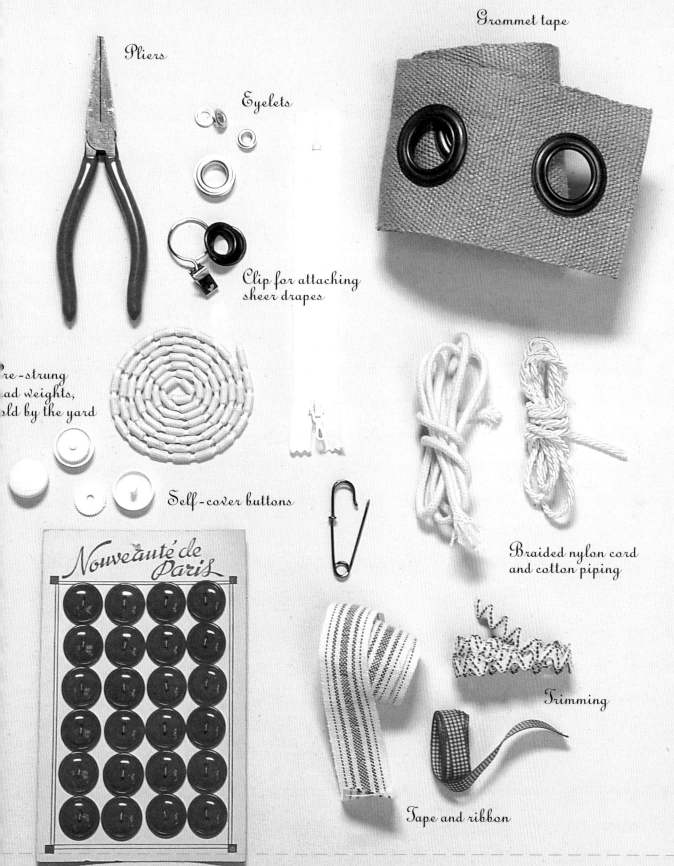

Pliers

Eyelets

Grommet tape

Clip for attaching sheer drapes

Pre-strung lead weights, sold by the yard

Self-cover buttons

Braided nylon cord and cotton piping

Nouveauté de Paris

Trimming

Tape and ribbon

Patterns and straight grains

Once you find and photocopy patterns that you like (e.g. sweet chemise, Bohemian flip flops, Azure Coast sun hat, lingerie carryall), enlarge them to fit your desired size for the finished project. For other items, refer to the step-by-step instructions and diagrams, armed with your tape measure and tailor's chalk.

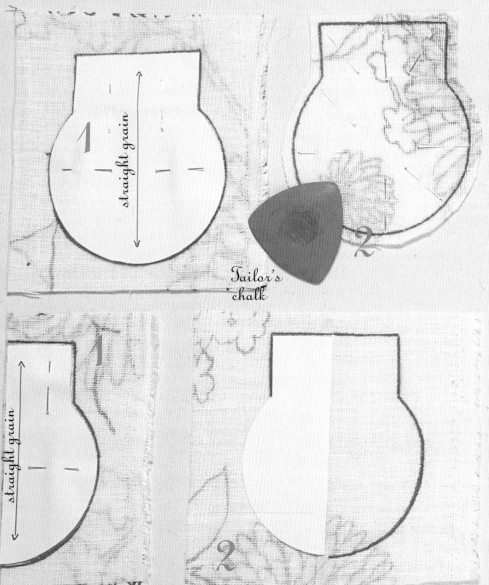

Tailor's chalk

For whole patterns

1
Pin the pattern onto the wrong side of double thickness of fabric (face right s of fabric together) and trace around t edge with tailor's chalk.

2
Cut ½ inch (1 cm) to the outside of the line for the seam allowance.

For half-patterns

1
Fold the fabric in two, pin the pattern to the wrong side of the fabric and tra around the edge with tailor's chalk.

2
Unfold the fabric, reverse the half-pattern and trace around the edge. Cut ½ inch (1 cm) to the outside of the line for the seam allowance.

Copying a pattern onto a piece of fabric

• Press the fabric. Working on a flat, well-protected surface, fold the fabric in half lengthwise, right sides together, and edge to edge.

• Position and pin the pattern making sure you match the straight grain of the fabric and the "straight grain" line marked on the pattern—the straight grain always runs parallel to the selvage of the fabric (see below).

• Pay particular attention to the direction of patterned fabrics (especially the joins) and the direction of the pile in plush fabrics such as velvet.

• Use tailor's chalk to draw freehand (or using a ruler for straight lines) around the edge of the pattern, then cut ½ inch (1 cm) to the outside of the line with sharp scissors.

• If you are using a half-pattern, make sure the pattern is copied symmetrically and that you've copied all the notches on the half-pattern (e.g. the opening at the bottom of the duvet cover).

What is the straight grain?

It's crucial to learn to recognize the direction of the straight grain when you're positioning a pattern, so that the fabric doesn't twist or hang crooked. The straight grain runs parallel to the selvages (the edges of the fabric that don't fray) and comprises the warp (lengthwise) threads. The weft (crosswise) threads run perpendicular to the warp and, if pulled, unravel the fabric. To place a pattern on the straight grain, align the straight grain arrow parallel with the selvage edge.

Always adjust your fabric before measuring . . .

Because cut fabric is never completely straight, it is essential to adjust the top and bottom ends to obtain a perfectly straight (crosswise) grain.

Make a slit in the selvage edge of the fabric, 1¼ inches (3 cm) from the two ends. Pull a crosswise thread and then re-cut the fabric along the line, or slit and tear the fabric if it is closely woven.

Buyer beware!

Always check that the quality of the fabric you're buying is consistent. If you're not sure, buy approximately an extra ½–1 yard (50 cm–1 meter), just in case.

2

Pull a crosswise thread and re-cut the fabric completely straight.

The sewing machine

Buying a machine

• Buy a portable machine—they take up less room, are much lighter, and the case usually contains such useful accessories as presser feet, machine oil, and so on.

• Choose a machine that does straight stitch for basic seams and zigzag for overstitching. By shortening the zigzag stitch length to almost zero, you obtain the satin stitch used for buttonholes and machine embroidery.

• Don't be afraid to ask for advice on different machine accessories, or to try them out in the store. Make sure you'll be able to get the machine repaired—the store may even run machine maintenance classes.

• Many specialist sewing-machine stores have reasonably priced second-hand models, which have been repaired and serviced in-store and are guaranteed for several months. This means you can try out your new hobby for a relatively small outlay.

How does it work?

A sewing machine uses two threads—the (upper) thread from the spool, which is intertwined with the (lower) thread from the bobbin as the needle pierces the fabric. The lowered presser foot holds the fabric onto the needle plate, which has two feed teeth that pull the fabric forward. Guide the fabric lightly with your hand (but don't hold onto it) as you sew to keep it moving forward. Put your foot on the pedal, and you're away!

Filling a bobbin

Ask how to fill the bobbin when you buy the machine. On some machines, there's a bobbin-winding mechanism on the upper machine, on others the bobbin is filled inside the machine beneath the needle plate.

Threading the machine

Follow the red thread in the picture opposite.

Threading the needle

Turn the wheel to raise the needle to its highest point, so that you can see the eye. Thread the needle from the grooved side (i.e. from front to back), pulling the thread through to a length of about 4 inches (10 cm).

Raising the bobbin thread

Insert the bobbin into the metal bobbin case (sometimes removable), leaving about 4 inches (10 cm) of thread, and fit the bobbin case back into the machine below the needle plate. Hold the upper (needle) thread to one side and turn the wheel (on the right) until the needle has gone down and up again. Pull gently on the upper thread to bring the bobbin thread out.

Special case—circular sewing

Remove the lower casing of the machine so that you can rotate the item being sewn. If the machine doesn't have a removable casing, place it so that it slightly overhangs the edge of the work surface. This will give you enough room to rotate the item, for example when sewing the Azure Coast sun hat together or topstitching the casing of the lingerie carryall.

First stitches and tricks of the trade

As the old adage goes: For better or for worse... There's no "worse" in sewing—
unless you're in a hurry. Precision and accuracy are the best guiding principles.
Take time to follow each step of the instructions, and you can't go wrong.

Practice makes perfect

Learn how to use your machine by practicing on pieces of cotton fabric (double thickness) on which you've drawn straight, parallel lines.

Make a backstitch (a few stitches forwards and backwards) at the beginning and end of each line of stitching as you'll need to do these later on your "real" seams.

Experiment by adjusting the stitch length for straight stitch, zigzag, and satin stitch.

Use another piece of fabric to sew curved lines, and practice varying the machine speed by depressing and releasing the foot control to get used to the difference.

Practice a little each day. Once you get used to it, you'll feel comfortable and at ease with your machine.

Straight stitch

This is the basic machine stitch. Make a backstitch (a few stitches forwards and backwards) at the beginning and end of each seam.

Adjust the stitch size to suit the thickness of the fabric—use shorter stitches for fine fabrics. The thicker the fabric, the longer the stitch needs to be.

To baste, you can use straight stitch at its maximum length and slightly loosen the tension of the upper thread. Don't make a backstitch so you can remove the stitching easily by pulling the thread on the underside of the seam.

Zigzag stitch

Zigzag stitch can be used in a number ways. You can adjust the length and wi as required for oversewing, or for edg buttonholes.

Oversew the fabric edges before pinni or basting together to prevent frayin Adjust the stitch length and width to the fabric—longer, more open stitche for thicker fabrics and shorter, closer stitches for fine ones. When oversewin the fabric should be held in the cente of the presser foot so that the zigzag along the edge. Alternatively, you can pinking shears for a quicker edge finis if the item is going to be lined.

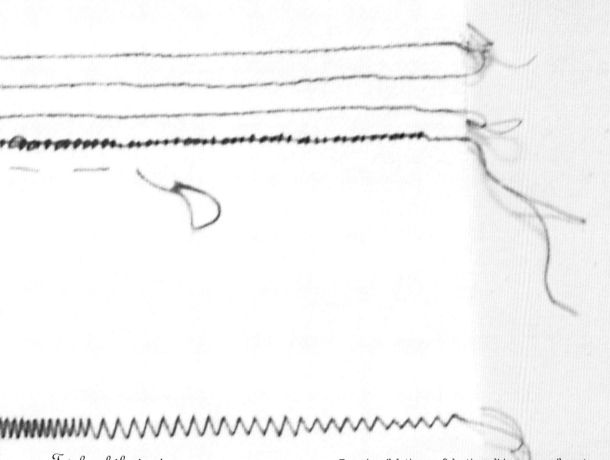

Tricks of the trade

• Use the same thread for threading the needle and winding the bobbin.

• Do a preliminary test on a piece of the fabric you'll be using to adjust the size of the stitches and tension of the thread (looser for thick fabrics and tighter for fine fabrics).

• Increase the size of the straight stitch on your machine to sew oilcloth, raffia, knitted, and thick fabrics, so as not to weaken or distort the textiles.

• To make oilcloth or soft leather slide more easily, or to prevent knitted fabrics from being pulled out of shape, place a sheet of tissue paper between the base of the machine and the fabric. You can also do this to keep fine fabrics from puckering while they are being sewn.

• You don't have to baste every item you're making. You can pin it together using extra-fine steel pins inserted at right angles to the line of the seam at ³/₄-inch (2-cm) intervals, and then machine the fabric directly. Before you start, make sure that the fabric is not wrinkled or puckered. Remove the pins as you sew.

If the stitching on a seam is irregular, check the tension of the thread

Before you begin a project, it's wise to adjust the tension of the upper thread and do a preliminary test on a piece of the fabric you'll be using. To adjust tension, turn the tension dial on the front of the machine higher for looser stitches and lower for tighter stitches.

• If the stitches are pulling too tightly on the right side of the fabric, causing it to wrinkle, there is too much tension on the upper thread. Move the tension dial to a higher number to loosen the thread.

• If the stitches are too loose on the wrong side of the fabric, causing it to wrinkle and forming visible loops, there is not enough tension on the upper thread. Move the tension dial to a lower number to tighten the thread.

Basic seams

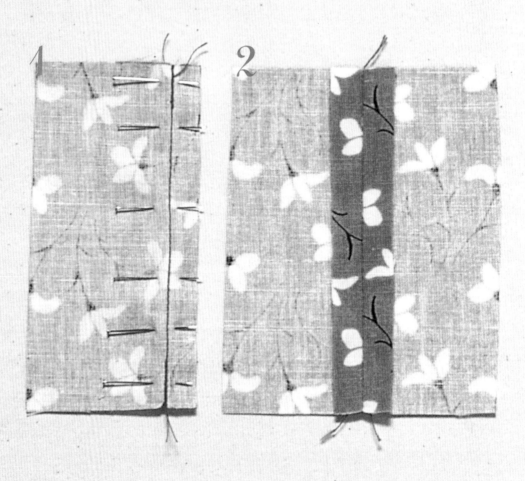

Single seam

1

Place the two pieces of fabric edge to edge, right sides together. Baste or pin (inserting the pins at right angles to the edge), and then stitch ½ inch (1 cm) from the edge of the fabric. Make a backstitch at the beginning and end of each seam.

2

Remove the basting or pins and press the seam flat on the wrong side of the fabric. Make sure you adjust the temperature of the iron to suit the fabric.

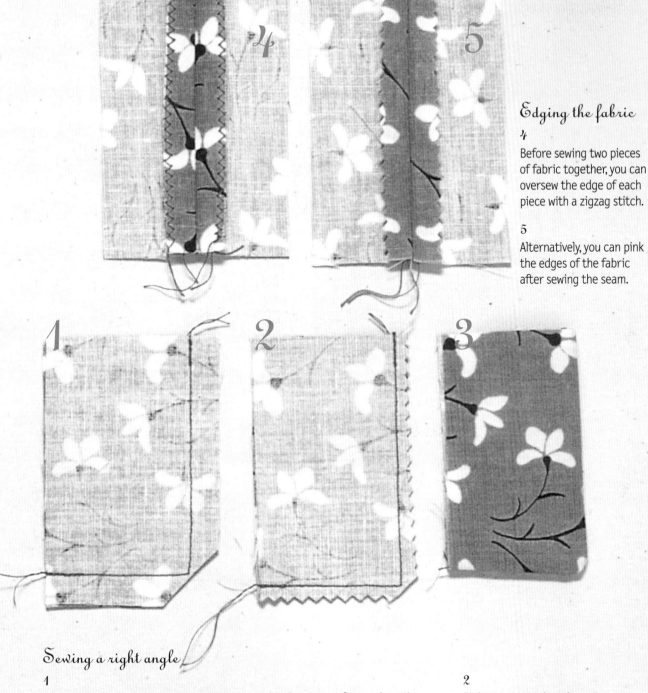

Edging the fabric

4

Before sewing two pieces of fabric together, you can oversew the edge of each piece with a zigzag stitch.

5

Alternatively, you can pink the edges of the fabric after sewing the seam.

Sewing a right angle

1

To sew an accurate right angle, stop at the end of the first seam—½ inch (1 cm) from the edge of the fabric—making sure the needle is still in the fabric. Raise the presser foot and turn the fabric 90°.

Lower the presser foot and continue to sew the second side of the angle. When the seam is finished, cut off the corner ⅟₁₂ inch (2 mm) from the seam.

2

Pink or oversew the edges.

3

Turn right side out and press (button-tufted cushion, wardrobe concierge, Paris opera wrap, duvet covers, etc.).

Curved seam and topstitching

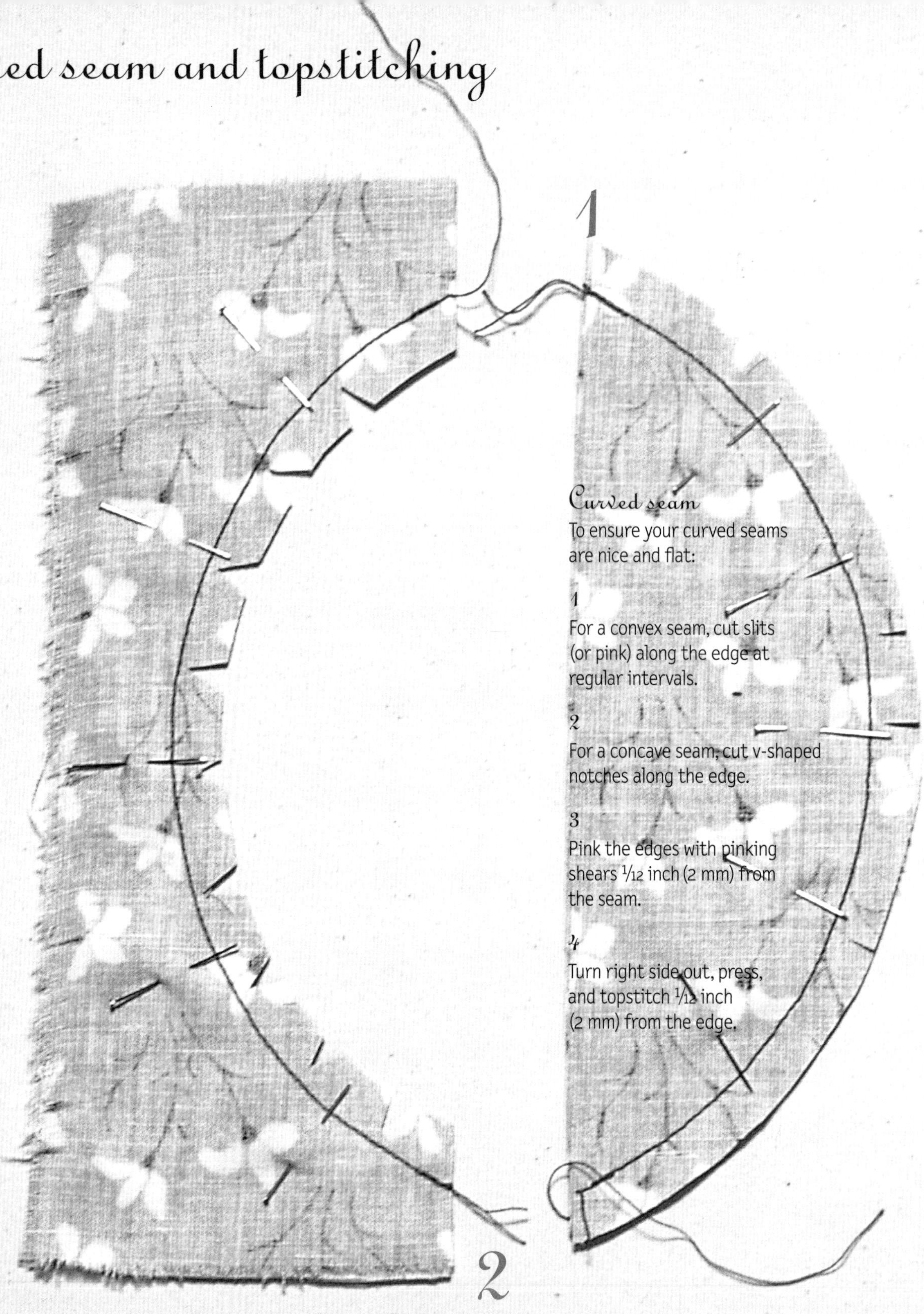

Curved seam

To ensure your curved seams are nice and flat:

1

For a convex seam, cut slits (or pink) along the edge at regular intervals.

2

For a concave seam, cut v-shaped notches along the edge.

3

Pink the edges with pinking shears $1/12$ inch (2 mm) from the seam.

4

Turn right side out, press, and topstitch $1/12$ inch (2 mm) from the edge.

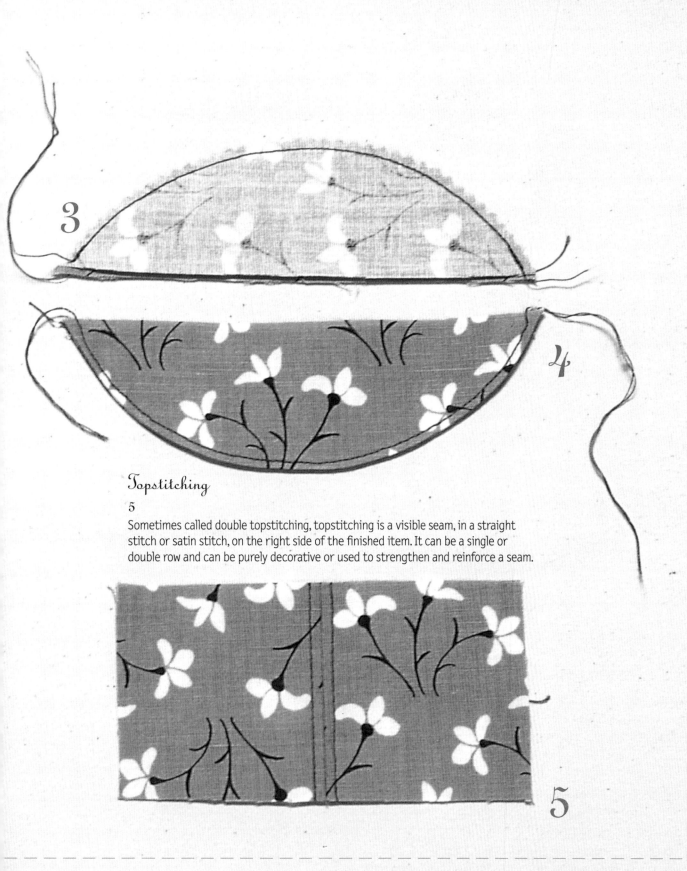

Topstitching

5

Sometimes called double topstitching, topstitching is a visible seam, in a straight stitch or satin stitch, on the right side of the finished item. It can be a single or double row and can be purely decorative or used to strengthen and reinforce a seam.

Flat seam

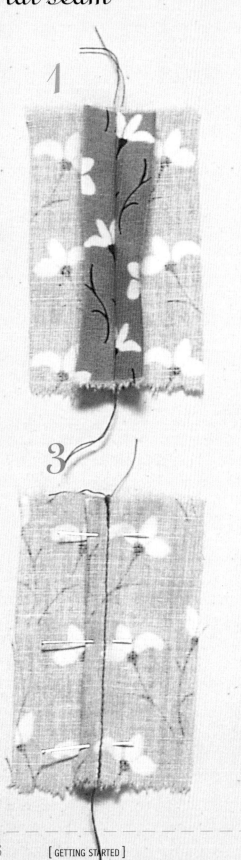

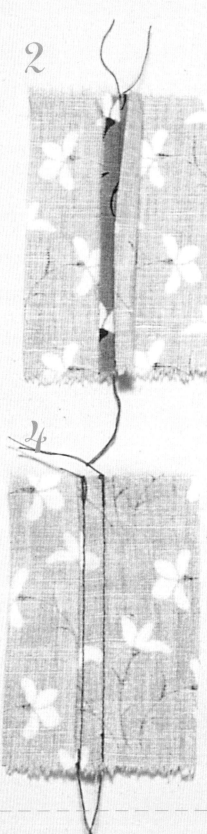

Flat seam

This is a particularly strong type of seam—ideal for items that will be frequently machine washed (e.g. the brasserie tablecloth).

1
Place the pieces of fabric edge to edge right sides together. Pin and then machine a single seam ½ inch (1 cm) from the edge of the fabric.

2
Press one edge of the seam flat and cut the other edge to ⅛ inch (3 mm).

3
Turn over a ¼-inch (5-mm) hem on the opposite (wider) edge and cover the narrower edge.

4
Pin and machine stitch 1/16 inch (1 mm) from the edge.

French seam

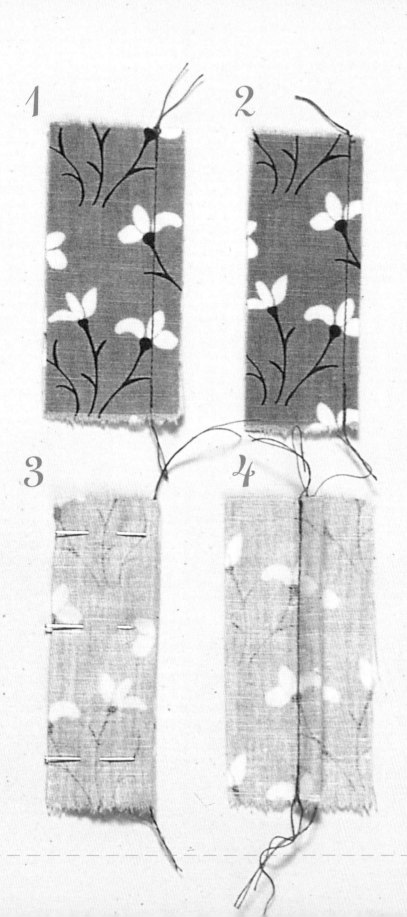

French seam

This type of seam is ideal for fine fabrics (such as the fabric used in the sweet chemise project on page 154).

1
Place the pieces of fabric edge to edge, wrong sides together. Pin and machine a single seam ½ inch (1 cm) from the edge of the fabric.

2
Trim the edges ⅛ inch (3 mm) from the seam.

3
Fold the fabric right sides together.

4
Machine stitch a second seam ¼ inch (5 mm) from the edge.

Hems

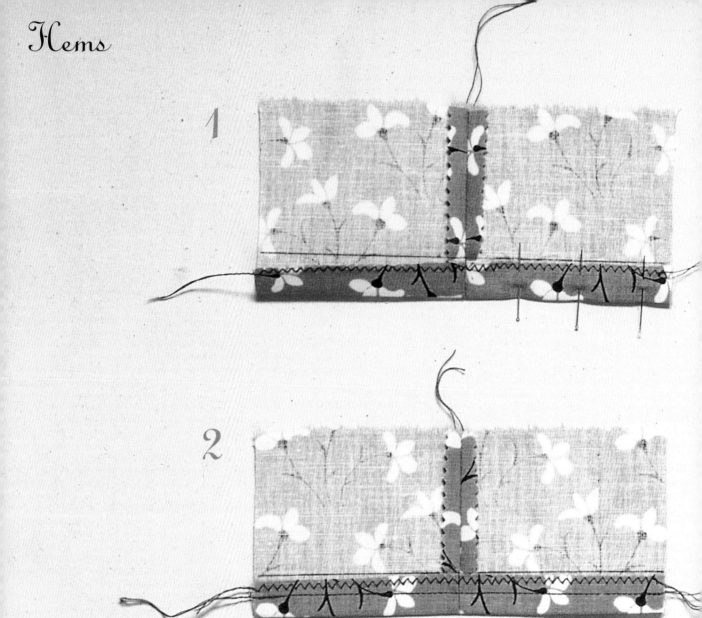

Single hem

For thick fabrics, you need only make a single hem (one fold) (as in the jacquard lampshade, page 106).

1

Oversew the edge of the fabric, draw a line ½ inch (1 cm) from the edge, fold the fabric along the line, and press the ½-inch (1-cm) hem on the wrong side of the fabric.

2

Make a line of straight stitch ¹⁄₁₂ inch (2 mm) from the edge.

Handy hint

To make sure your hems are even, draw a pencil line on the wrong side of the fabric as a guide for single hems, and draw two lines for double hems and turned-under hems, depending on their width. It's best to press hems before pinning and sewing by hand or machine.

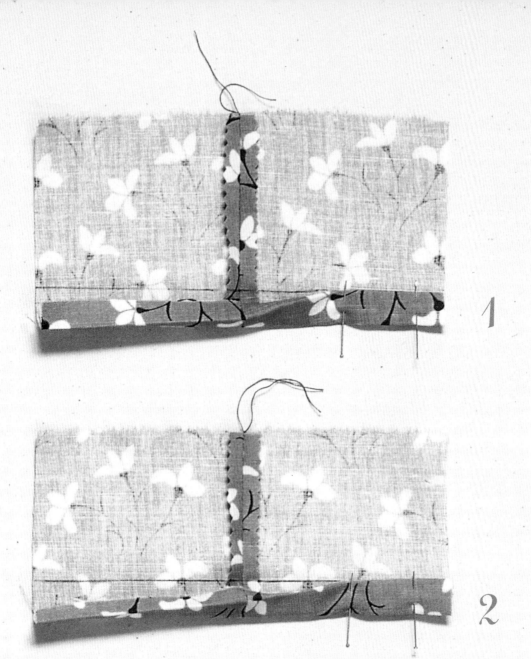

1

2

Double hem—1/2 inch (1 cm)

This gives a firm hem for fabrics with a medium or fine texture (e.g. brasserie tablecloth, sweet chemise).

1

Draw two lines, the first ¾ inch (2 cm) and the second 1¼ inches (3 cm) from the edge of the fabric. Fold the fabric twice on the wrong side. Press the hem.

Pin and stitch on the wrong side of the fabric, ¹⁄₁₂ inch (2 mm) from the edge of the hem.

Turned-under hem—1/2 inch (1 cm)

2

The turned-under hem is a variation on the double hem, used for fabrics with a medium or thick texture (e.g. wraparound robe, grommetted drapes). The proportions of the size of the fold to the hem are wider—½ inch to 4 inches (1 cm to 10 cm)—the fold being narrower than the hem to prevent it being too bulky.

Mitered and non-mitered corners

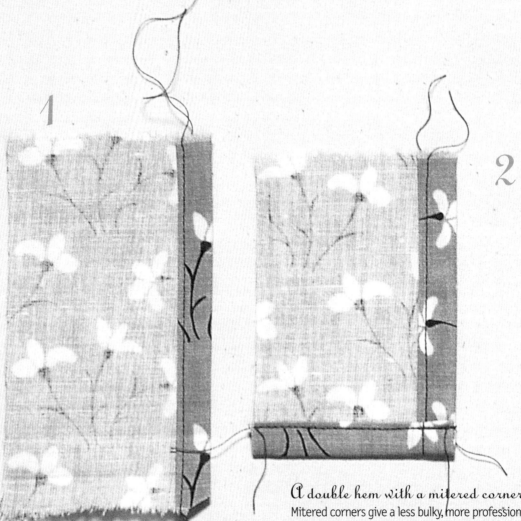

Non-mitered corners

The corner formed at the junction of two hems can be mitered or non-mitered.

1

Make a double hem along one of the sides, fold the hem on the second side, press, and cut off the corner.

2

Fold the second hem and sew as for the first, ending with a backstitch.

A double hem with a mitered corner

Mitered corners give a less bulky, more professional finish. If you're working on fine fabric, make a narrow double hem — ½ inch (1 cm). For thicker fabrics, it's better to make a wider turned-under hem, ½ inch to 4 inches (1 cm to 10 cm).

1

Fold the fabric to the required width for both hems, and press.

2

Unfold, draw a line across the corner, and cut the corner ½ inch (1 cm) to the outside of the line.

3

Fold the corner along the line, fold the sides twice, and pin.

4

Sew the hem ¹⁄₁₂ inch (2 mm) from the edge.

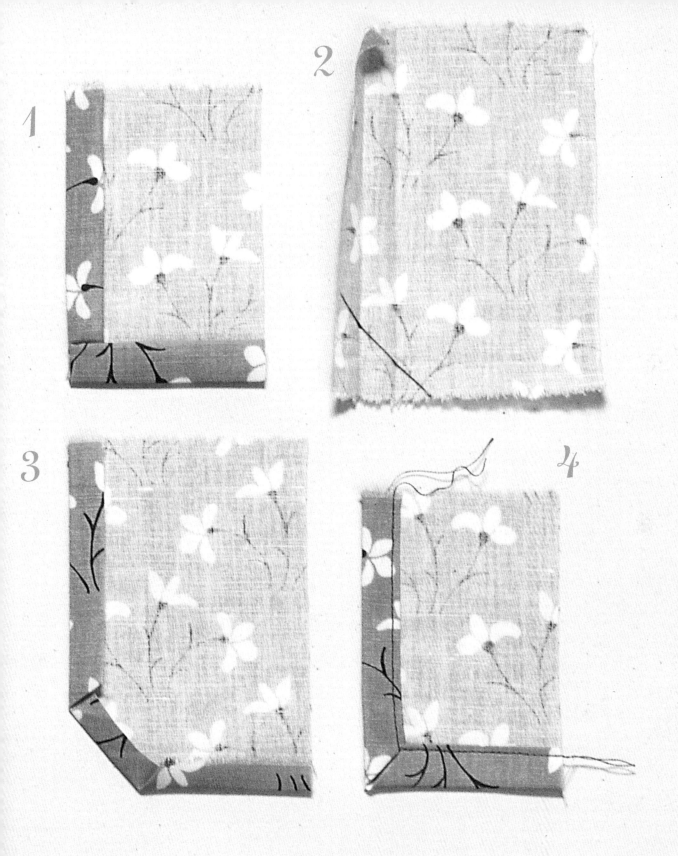

Bias binding

Edging with bias binding

Bias binding can be used to cover the edges of the fabric and provide straight or curved edging (e.g. Saturday market caddy, garden-artist's apron).

1
Place the bias binding and fabric edge to edge and right sides together. Sew at ¼ inch (5 mm) from the edge (inside the fold).

2
Fold the binding onto the wrong side of the fabric.

3
Make a line of machine stitching ¹⁄₁₂ inch (2 mm) from the edge (or hand stitch on the wrong side of the fabric using running stitch).

4
You can also baste by hand before making a single line of stitching.

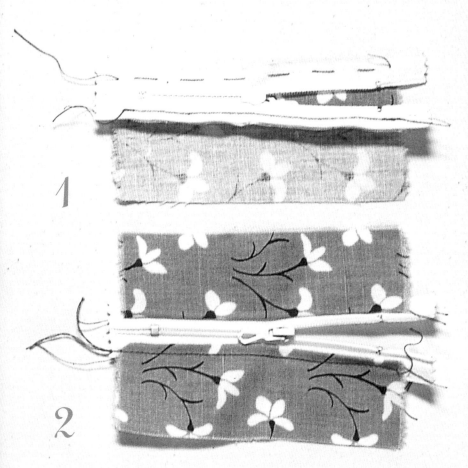

Putting in a zipper

There are various ways of putting in a zipper. The method shown here (used for the chic cosmetic case and furnishing fabric bean bag) is simple and ideal for beginners.

Make sure the zipper is in the same material (cotton or synthetic) and color as your fabric. For large items, like the furnishing fabric bean bag, you can buy zippers by the yard.

Close the zipper before you start sewing, and change the presser foot. The operation will be much simpler if you use the zipper foot. If you don't have a special zipper foot, stop midway through machining, making sure the needle is still in the fabric (as for sewing a right angle, page 23), open the zipper, and carry on stitching.

1

Place the zipper and fabric edge to edge and right sides together. Baste or pin the zipper to the fabric and sew ¼ inch (5 mm) from the edge. Repeat on the other side of the zipper.

2

Turn the right way around and press. You can always make a line of top-stitching so that the zipper is more secure.

Buttonholes and self-cover buttons

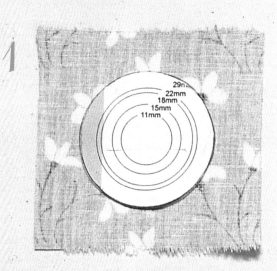

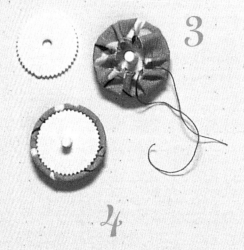

Covering buttons

These are attractive and very easy to do, and they add a touch of style and sophistication to your projects.

1
Cut the template provided on the package to the size of the button, and draw around it onto the fabric.

2
Cut the disk of fabric and baste around the edge.

3
Place the button in the center of the fabric circle, then tighten and knot the basting thread to hold the gathers in place.

4
Fix the back of the button and press into place. That's all there is to it!

Buttonholes

Mark the position of the buttonholes with a single line. If you're using thick fabric, make a slit with embroidery scissors and then edge the buttonhole with shortened, but fairly broad zigzag stitch. Do a secure finishing-off stitch at each end. This type of shortened zigzag stitch (set almost at zero) is known as satin stitch. It can also be used for machine embroidery.

On some machines you can automatic make buttonholes by pre-setting the dimensions, and the machine does the rest. This method requires a special buttonhole foot, and the fabric is slit after the buttonholes have been stitched. You can also hand stitch buttonholes by edging them with blanket stitch like your grandmothers used to do.

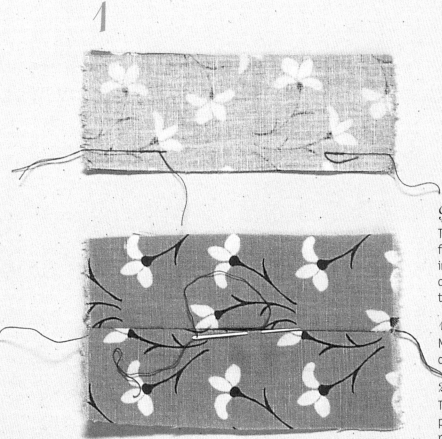

1

2

Running stitch by hand

This invisible stitch is ideal for sewing folded edges or hand stitching openings in articles such as slippers, throws, and cushions. Just make sure your thread is the same color as the fabric.

1

Make a backstitch at each end of the opening.

2

Turn the article the right way out and press the opening. Hand stitch with running stitch, catching the two pieces of fabric alternately, and running the thread ¼ inch (5 mm) inside the folds of the opening.

First steps

38 [INSTRUCTIONS PAGE 50]

Provençal poppy lampshade

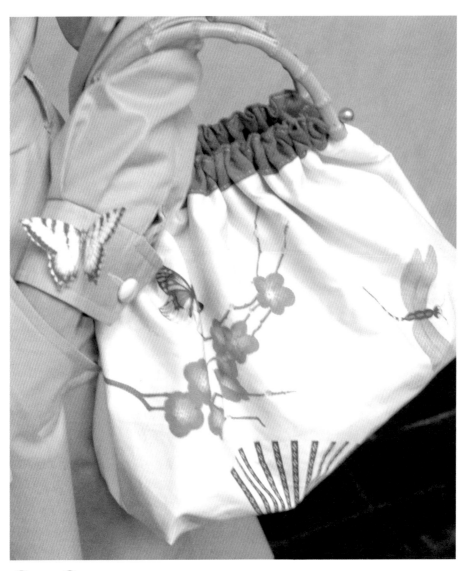

Rive Gauche carryall

Colette screen

Boulevard butterfly trench

French wool beret

Tasseled shoe tote

Monet flower brooch

[INSTRUCTIONS PAGE 48]

Tasseled shoe tote

If you want to take your favorite shoes away with you for a weekend on the Côte d'Azur, but are worried the soles might not be entirely clean, protect them—and the rest of your clothes—with this attractive shoe tote.

Shopping list

- ½ YD (50 CM) PLAIN FABRIC, 54 INCHES (140 CM) WIDE
- REMNANT OF PATTERNED FABRIC, AT LEAST 15½ x 14½ INCHES (39 x 37 CM)
- 1 YARD (1 M) CORD
- 2 MATCHING TASSELS (FOR TRIMMING CORD)
- FABRIC GLUE

Sewing box

- TAILOR'S CHALK
- TAPE MEASURE OR RULER
- PINS
- DRESSMAKING SCISSORS
- MATCHING THREAD
- SAFETY PIN
- SEWING NEEDLE

1

Draw (with chalk and ruler) and cut out two rectangles 18 x 14½ inches (45 x 37 cm) and one rectangle 15½ x 14½ inches (39 x 37 cm) from the plain fabric, and one rectangle 15½ x 14½ inches (39 x 37 cm) from the patterned fabric. Place the two pairs of matching rectangles (i.e. with the same dimensions) right sides together and pin edge to edge.

Machine in straight stitch ½ inch (1 cm) from the edges (see diagrams), leaving the openings—4 inches (10 cm) at the bottom and ⅝ inch (1.5 cm) near the top—in the lining bag. Cut off the bottom corners of each rectangle [diagram 1.a]. Turn the cover bag right side out and slip it inside the lining bag, right sides together [diagram 1.b].

2

With the top of the bags edge to edge, pin the opening around the top of the cover bag, making sure you open out the side seams. Machine a circular seam ½ inch (1 cm) from the edge in straight stitch.

3

Turn the bag right side out through the opening at the bottom of the lining, positioning the lining inside the bag. Press the edge of the casing formed at the top of the cover by the extra length of the lining, and topstitch 1/12 inch (2 mm) from the top and bottom edges using straight stitch [diagram 3]. Close the opening at the bottom of the lining by hand with running stitch.

Using the safety pin, thread the cord through the casing. Fix the tassels to each end of the cord using fabric glue and secure them with a few hand stitches.

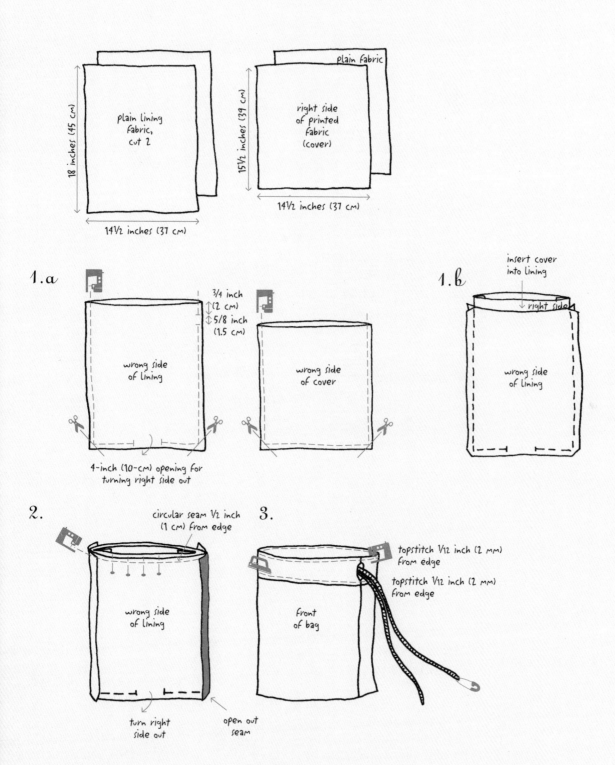

plain lining fabric, cut 2

18 inches (45 cm)

14½ inches (37 cm)

plain fabric

right side of printed fabric (cover)

15½ inches (39 cm)

14½ inches (37 cm)

1.a

¾ inch (2 cm)
5/8 inch (1.5 cm)

wrong side of lining

wrong side of cover

4-inch (10-cm) opening for turning right side out

1.b

insert cover into lining

right side

wrong side of lining

2.

circular seam ½ inch (1 cm) from edge

wrong side of lining

turn right side out

open out seam

3.

topstitch 1/12 inch (2 mm) from edge

topstitch 1/12 inch (2 mm) from edge

front of bag

Monet flower brooch

Delightful and so easy to make!

Shopping list

- REMNANT OF FABRIC WITH A PRINTED FLOWER MOTIF
- IRON-ON INTERFACING (NONWOVEN)
- 1 METAL BROOCH MOUNT
- FABRIC GLUE

Sewing box

- SMALL SCISSORS

Tool box

- CRAFT KNIFE AND CUTTING BOARD

1

Cut out two rectangles of the same size, one of the flower print and one from the iron-on interfacing [diagram 1.a]. Place the adhesive (shiny) side of the iron-on fabric against the wrong side of the flower motif, and fuse them by pressing with a hot iron. Let cool. Cut around the edge of the flower motif with the small scissors [diagram 1.b].

2

Place the motif on the cutting board and, using the craft knife, carefully cut around the edge of some of the petals to make them stand out (fold lightly by hand) creating a three-dimensional look.

3

Stick the metal brooch mount to the back of the flower using the fabric glue.

1.a

iron-on interfacing, adhesive side

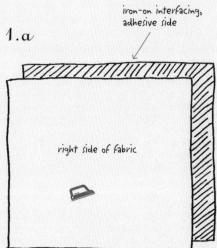

right side of fabric

1.b

right side of fabric

right side of fabric

2.

cut out a few petals with the craft knife

3.

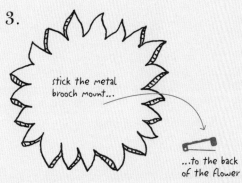

stick the metal brooch mount...

...to the back of the flower

Provençal poppy lampshade

Flick a switch and set the mood with this soothing scarlet shade.

Shopping list

- 1 RECTANGLE OF DRAPERY FABRIC CUT
  TO THE SIZE OF THE LAMPSHADE PLUS
  SEAM ALLOWANCES
- 1 ROUND LAMPSHADE

Sewing box

- DRESSMAKING SCISSORS
- TAPE MEASURE
- RULER
- TAILOR'S CHALK
- MATCHING THREAD
- PINS

1

Measure the lampshade with the
tape measure and add 2 inches (5 cm)
to the height and 1 inch (2 cm) to the
diameter.

2

Press the fabric and then draw and
cut out the rectangle [diagram 2.a].
Draw lines on the long sides to mark
the folds of the ½-inch (1-cm) double
hems [diagram 2.b]. Fold and press
the double hems, then unfold.

3

With right sides together and edge to
edge, pin and machine the short sides
of the rectangle ½ inch (1 cm) from
the edge [diagram 3.a]. Open out the
seam and press. Fold and pin the
double hems. Machine a double row
of topstitching 1/16 inch (1 mm) from
the top and bottom edges of the
hem—see diagram [diagram 3.b].
Turn the cover right side out and
place over the lampshade, matching
seam to seam.

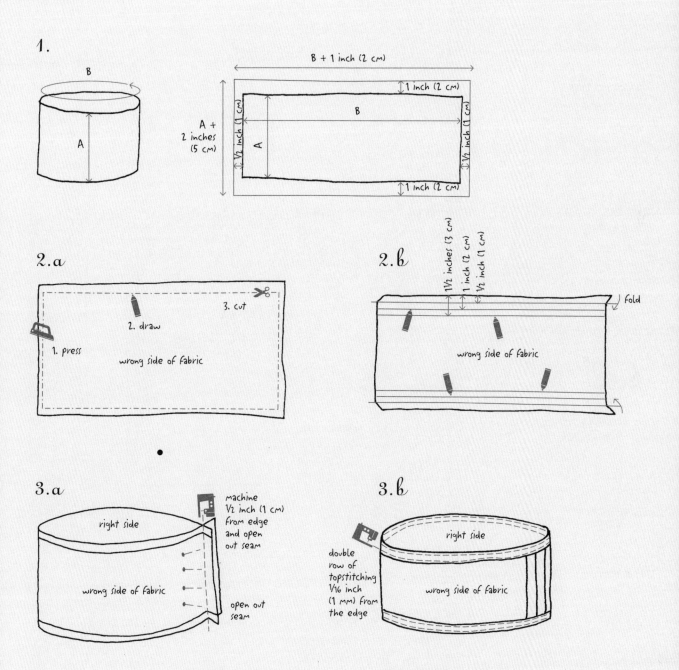

1.

B

A

B + 1 inch (2 cm)

1 inch (2 cm)

½ inch (1 cm)

B

A

A +
2 inches
(5 cm)

½ inch (1 cm)

1 inch (2 cm)

2.a

3. cut

2. draw

1. press

wrong side of fabric

2.b

1½ inches (3 cm)
1 inch (2 cm)
½ inch (1 cm)

fold

wrong side of fabric

3.a

right side

wrong side of fabric

machine
½ inch (1 cm)
from edge
and open
out seam

open out
seam

3.b

double
row of
topstitching
1/16 inch
(1 mm) from
the edge

right side

wrong side of fabric

Colette screen

Shopping list

- 1³/₄ YARDS (160 CM) DRAPERY FABRIC, 54 INCHES (140 CM) WIDE
- 6 LENGTHS OF WOOD: 1³/₄ X 1 X 67 INCHES (4.5 X 2.5 X 170 CM)
- 6 LENGTHS OF WOOD: 1³/₄ X 1 X 18 INCHES (4.5 X 2.5 X 45 CM)
- 6 WOODEN DOWELS 1/2 INCH (1 CM) DIAMETER X 19 INCHES (48 CM) LONG
- 6 SPLIT HINGES, 2 X 1¹/₂ INCHES (5 X 4 CM)
- 12 SCREWS FOR THE SCREEN PANELS
- 36 SCREWS FOR THE SPLIT HINGES
- SANDPAPER
- PAINT FOR THE WOOD

Sewing box

- TAILOR'S CHALK
- ERASABLE MARKER
- TAPE MEASURE AND LONG RULER
- PINS
- MATCHING THREAD

Tool box

- DRILL WITH A NO. 10 BIT FOR WOOD
- PAINT BRUSH

1

Press, draw, and cut out three rectangles 60¹/₂ x 18 inches (154 x 46 cm) from the fabric [diagram 1.a]. On the long sides, draw and press the ¹/₂-inch (1-cm) double hems, then machine in straight stitch ¹/₁₆ inch (1 mm) from the edge [diagram 1.b]. On the short sides, draw and press the 1-inch (2.5-cm) turned-under hems—⁵/₈ inch (1.5 cm) for the turn plus 1 inch (2.5 cm) for the hem. These will form the casings for the dowels. Machine in straight stitch ¹/₁₆ inch (1 mm) from the edge [diagram 1.c].

2

Cut or get a joiner to cut the lengths of wood and dowels. Using a no. 10 bit, drill holes for the dowels in the 67-inch (170-cm) lengths of wood [diagram 2.a]. It's important to drill at right angles to the wood—to help you do this, place a wooden block against the drill bit. Drill to a depth of 1 inch (2.5 cm) so you can slot in the dowels [diagram 2.b].

3

Assemble the frames by pre-drilling and screwing the four lengths of wood together [diagram 3.a]. Screw on the split hinges and paint the framework (2 coats). Sand the ends of the dowels with the sandpaper and then paint (1 coat). Let dry for 24 hours.

Feed the dowels through the casing of the fabric panels and then slot into the holes in the framework [diagram 3.b].

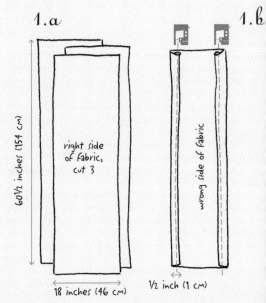

1.a

1.b

60¹/₂ inches (154 cm)

right side of fabric, cut 3

wrong side of fabric

18 inches (46 cm)

¹/₂ inch (1 cm)

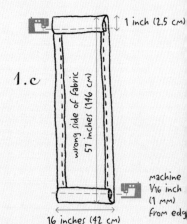

1 inch (2.5 cm)

1.c

wrong side of fabric

57 inches (146 cm)

machine ¹/₁₆ inch (1 mm) from edge

16 inches (42 cm)

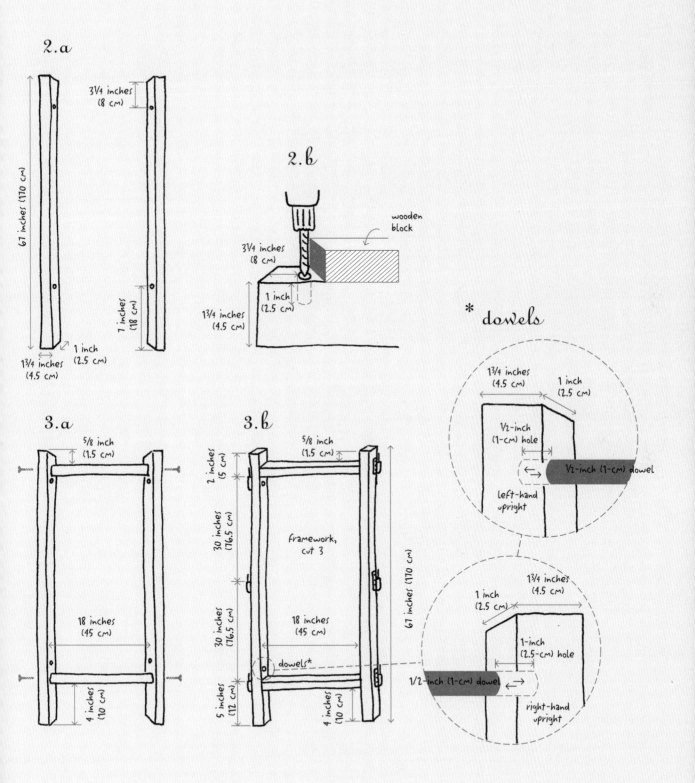

2.a

67 inches (170 cm)

3¼ inches (8 cm)

7 inches (18 cm)

1 inch (2.5 cm)

1¾ inches (4.5 cm)

2.b

wooden block

3¼ inches (8 cm)

1 inch (2.5 cm)

1¾ inches (4.5 cm)

* dowels

1¾ inches (4.5 cm)

1 inch (2.5 cm)

½-inch (1-cm) hole

½-inch (1-cm) dowel

left-hand upright

1 inch (2.5 cm)

1¾ inches (4.5 cm)

1-inch (2.5-cm) hole

½-inch (1-cm) dowel

right-hand upright

3.a

5/8 inch (1.5 cm)

18 inches (45 cm)

4 inches (10 cm)

3.b

5/8 inch (1.5 cm)

2 inches (5 cm)

30 inches (76.5 cm)

framework, cut 3

30 inches (76.5 cm)

18 inches (45 cm)

67 inches (170 cm)

dowels*

5 inches (12 cm)

4 inches (10 cm)

Boulevard butterfly trench

Liven up a passé trench coat with a little imagination!

Shopping list

- VINTAGE TRENCH COAT
- SELF-COVER BUTTONS THE SAME SIZE
  AS THE ORIGINAL BUTTONS
- REMNANTS OF FABRIC WITH PRINTED MOTIFS
  (BUTTERFLIES, FLOWERS) AND STRIPES FOR
  THE BUTTONS
- IRON-ON INTERFACING (NONWOVEN)

Sewing box

- ERASABLE MARKER
- SMALL SCISSORS
- MATCHING THREAD

1

Remove the original buttons from the trench coat. You can either have the replacement buttons covered professionally or you can cover them yourself (see page 34). Sew the new buttons on by hand.

2

Cut out two rectangles of the same size from the printed and iron-on interfacing. Place the adhesive (shiny) side of the iron-on fabric against the wrong side of the butterfly or flower motif, and fuse by pressing with a hot iron [diagram 2.a]. Let cool. Cut around the edge of the motif with the small scissors [diagram 2.b]. Do the same for the other motifs.

3

Sew on the motifs by hand so that the stitching is invisible.

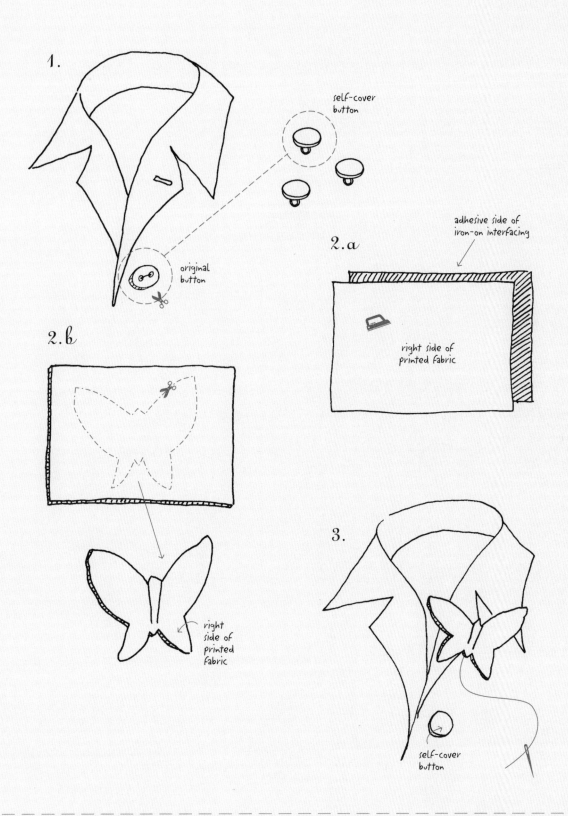

1.

self-cover
button

original
button

2.a

adhesive side of
iron-on interfacing

right side of
printed fabric

2.b

right
side of
printed
fabric

3.

self-cover
button

Rive Gauche carryall

Simply delightful!

Shopping list

- ½ YARD (50 CM) PRINTED FABRIC, 48 INCHES (120 CM) WIDE
- ½ YARD (50 CM) PLAIN-COLORED FABRIC, 48 INCHES (120 CM) WIDE
- 2 X BAMBOO HANDLES, 8 INCHES (20 CM) IN DIAMETER
- THREADED METAL ROD, ⅛ INCH (3 MM) DIAMETER X 20 INCHES (50 CM) LONG
- 4 ROUND SCREW-ON ENDS FOR THE THREADED RODS

Sewing box

- TAILOR'S CHALK
- TAPE MEASURE OR RULER
- SEWING NEEDLE
- PINS
- MATCHING THREAD
- DRESSMAKING SCISSORS

Tool box

- WIRE CUTTERS
- METAL FILE
- DRILL WITH A SMALL-GAUGE BIT

1

Draw two rectangles 14 x 22 inches (35 x 55 cm) on the printed fabric and two more 17 x 22 inches (42 x 55 cm) on the plain lining fabric. Cut out.

2

Pin each pair of rectangles, right sides together and edge to edge. Mark the openings and machine ½ inch (1 cm) from the edge [diagram 2.a]. Do the same for the lining, leaving a 10-inch (25-cm) opening at the bottom [diagram 2.b].

3

To make the corners at the bottom of the bag, machine a seam between 4½ and 2½ inches (12–6 cm) from the point of the bottom corners, then cut off the corners ½ inch (1 cm) from the seam. Do the same for the lining.

4

Turn the lining right side out and insert into the bag so that the right side of the lining is facing the right side of the bag. Pin the two side openings and machine ½-inch (1-cm) from the edge along the sides of each opening for 3 inches (8 cm), stopping ½ inch (1 cm) from the top edge. Make a ¹⁄₁₂-inch (2-mm) slit at the base of each side opening [diagram 4].

5

With right sides together and edge to edge, pin together the top edges of the bag and lining [diagram 5.a] and machine ½ inch (1 cm) from the edge. Turn right side out through the opening. Press the casing formed by the extra length of lining, then pin and top-stitch ¹⁄₁₂ inch (2 mm) from the top and bottom edges [diagram 5.b]. Drill a small hole through the end of the handles with a small-gauge bit and, using wire cutters, cut the threaded rod to the interior diameter of the handles plus 1½ inches (4 cm). File the ends of the rods and thread through the handles and the casings, spreading the gathers evenly. Secure by attaching the screw-on ends. Close the opening in the lining by hand with running stitch.

1.

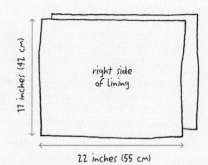

right side of fabric front of bag

14 inches (35 cm)

22 inches (55 cm)

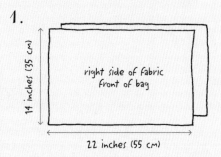

right side of lining

17 inches (42 cm)

22 inches (55 cm)

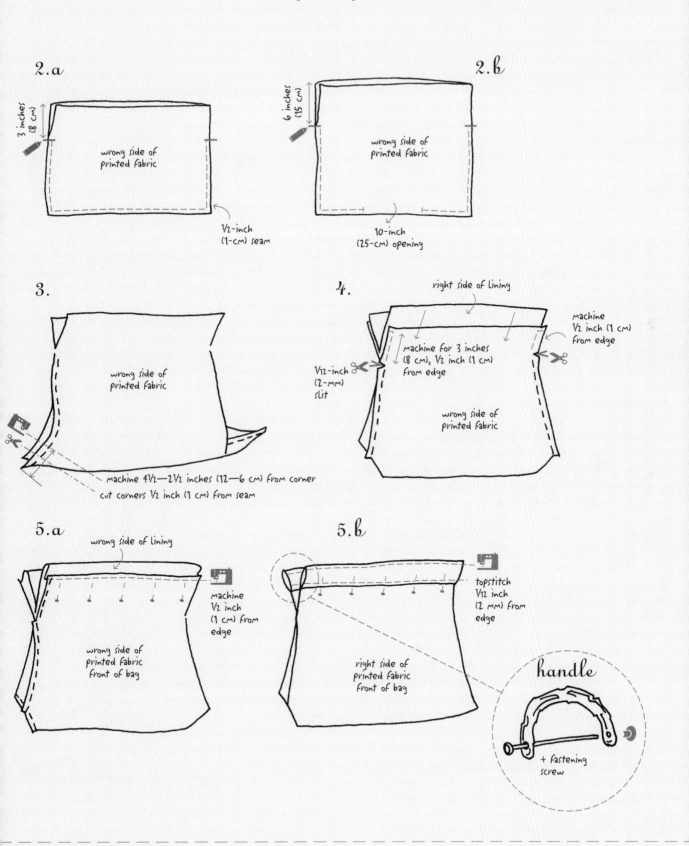

2.a

3 inches (8 cm)

wrong side of printed fabric

½-inch (1-cm) seam

2.b

6 inches (15 cm)

wrong side of printed fabric

10-inch (25-cm) opening

3.

wrong side of printed fabric

machine 4½—2½ inches (12—6 cm) from corner

cut corners ½ inch (1 cm) from seam

4.

right side of lining

machine ½ inch (1 cm) from edge

machine for 3 inches (8 cm), ½ inch (1 cm) from edge

1/12-inch (2-mm) slit

wrong side of printed fabric

5.a

wrong side of lining

machine ½ inch (1 cm) from edge

wrong side of printed fabric front of bag

5.b

topstitch 1/12 inch (2 mm) from edge

right side of printed fabric front of bag

handle

+ fastening screw

French wool beret

Sometimes you should just let things go to your head!

Shopping list

- A BLANKET (E.G. AN OLD GREY WOOL BLANKET), OR POLAR FLEECE, FELT, OR BOILED WOOL

Sewing box

- DRESSMAKING SCISSORS
- RULER
- TAILOR'S CHALK
- THICK THREAD IN A LIGHTER SHADE THAN THE BLANKET FABRIC
- PINS
- COMPASSES
- 2 SHEETS PAPER, 12 X 17 INCHES

1

Measure the circumference of your head with a tape measure [diagram 1.a]. Cut out a rectangle to the length of this measurement plus 1 inch (2 cm) (for seam allowance) x 2 inches (5 cm). Topstitch ¼ inch (5 mm) from one of the long sides using medium-length straight stitch [diagram 1.b]. Machine the two short ends together ½ inch (1 cm) from the edge, right sides together and edge to edge [diagram 1.c]. Press the seam flat.

2

Using a pair of compasses, draw the patterns for the two sections of the beret onto the sheets of paper. Cut them out, pin onto the fabric, and draw around them with the tailor's chalk. Cut the two circles out of the fabric, then cut another (smaller) circle with a diameter of 6¼ inches (16 cm) out of the center of one of the circles.

3

Pin the two circles of fabric, wrong sides together and edge to edge. Topstitch ¼ inch (5 mm) from the edge using medium-length straight stitch so that the stitching is clearly visible.

4

Pin the non-topstiched side of the head band to the inside of the inner circle, wrong sides together and edge to edge. Topstitch ¼ inch (5 mm) from the edge using medium-length straight stitch so that the stitching is clearly visible. Turn the band right side out so that it is on the outside of the beret [diagram 5].

5

For the "stalk" on top of the beret, cut out a rectangle of fabric 1½ x 2½ inches (4 x 6 cm). Roll tightly and handstitch with running stitch. Sew securely in the center of the crown.

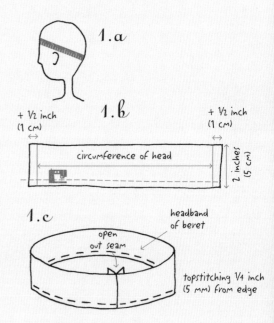

1.a

1.b

+ ½ inch (1 cm)

+ ½ inch (1 cm)

circumference of head

2 inches (5 cm)

1.c

open out seam

headband of beret

topstitching ¼ inch (5 mm) from edge

2.

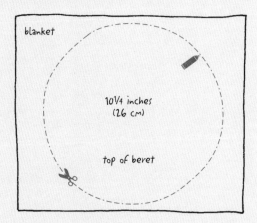

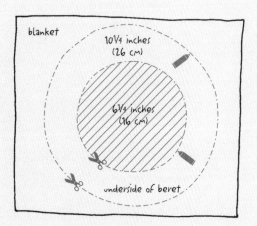

blanket

10¼ inches
(26 cm)

top of beret

blanket

10¼ inches
(26 cm)

6¼ inches
(16 cm)

underside of beret

3.

4.

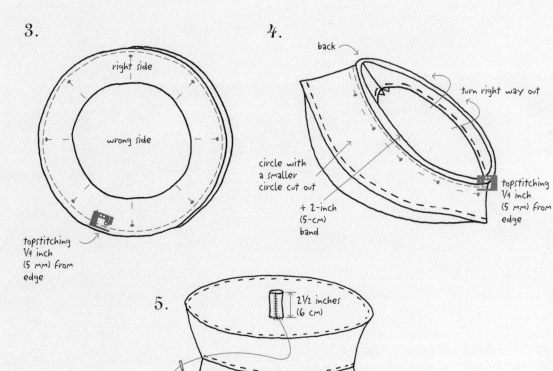

right side

wrong side

topstitching
¼ inch
(5 mm) from
edge

back

turn right way out

circle with
a smaller
circle cut out

+ 2-inch
(5-cm)
band

topstitching
¼ inch
(5 mm) from
edge

5.

2½ inches
(6 cm)

sew with
running stitch

The nesting instinct

Velvet striped rug

[INSTRUCTIONS PAGE 70]

Button-backed gallery chair

[INSTRUCTIONS PAGE 72]

Grommetted drapes

French cotton table runner

[INSTRUCTIONS PAGE 74]

Button-tufted cushion

Versailles velvet ottoman

[INSTRUCTIONS PAGE 76]

Paris opera wrap

[INSTRUCTIONS PAGE 78]

Velvet striped rug

Shopping list

- 40 INCHES (100 CM) STRIPED UPHOLSTERY
  FABRIC, 54 INCHES (140 CM) WIDE
  (WE USED A LINEN AND VELVET STRIPED
  FABRIC)
- 26½ YARDS (24.5 M) CHAIR WEBBING,
  3½ INCHES (9 CM) WIDE

Sewing box

- TAILOR'S CHALK OR DRESSMAKER'S
  WHITE MARKING PENCIL
- LONG RULER
- PINS
- DRESSMAKING SCISSORS
- HEAVY-DUTY MATCHING THREAD
- SEWING NEEDLE

1

Cut out five strips, 8 inches (20 cm) wide, from the upholstery fabric. When cutting, bear in mind that the strips will be joined on the long sides, so cut the fabric ½ inch (1 cm) from a stripe to create an invisible seam. If necessary, remember to subtract the width of the selvages when measuring lengths of fabric. Leave two of the strips at 54 inches (140 cm), cut another two of the strips to 52 inches (132 cm) and cut the final strip into two pieces, each 14 inches (37 cm) long.

2

Cut the webbing into 14 strips of 69 inches (175 cm). Test the zigzag stitch on your machine, and check the tension of the thread on a piece of webbing. Then machine all the strips of webbing together edge to edge using medium-length zigzag stitch, making a backstitch at each end of the strips. Press the surface of the webbing.

3

Pin the two sections that will form the long sides of the rug (the longest and the shortest strips), right sides together and edge to edge. Machine ½ inch (1 cm) from the edge using medium-length straight stitch, then open out and press the seam [diagram 3.a]. Draw a line along one of the long sides, on the wrong side of the fabric and 1 inch (2 cm) from the edge, then press a ½-inch (1-cm) fold for the turned-under hem [diagram 3.b]. Pin this long strip onto the stitched webbing center of the rug, right sides together and 3 inches (8 cm) from the edge, then machine ½ inch (1 cm) from the edge using medium-length straight stitch. Repeat for the other long side of the rug [diagram 3.c].

4

Turn the rug over. Fold and pin the edging strips of upholstery fabric onto the wrong side of the rug, and machine stitch ⅛ inch (3 mm) from the edge.

5

Repeat steps 3 and 4 for the short sides, remembering to overlap 1 inch (2 cm) at each end of the strips of upholstery fabric. Before machining the second seam ⅛ inch (3 mm) from the edge, turn the ends of the strips of fabric under onto the wrong side. Pin and then handstitch the corners with running stitch. Machine the second seam ⅛ inch (3 mm) from the edge on the wrong side of the rug.

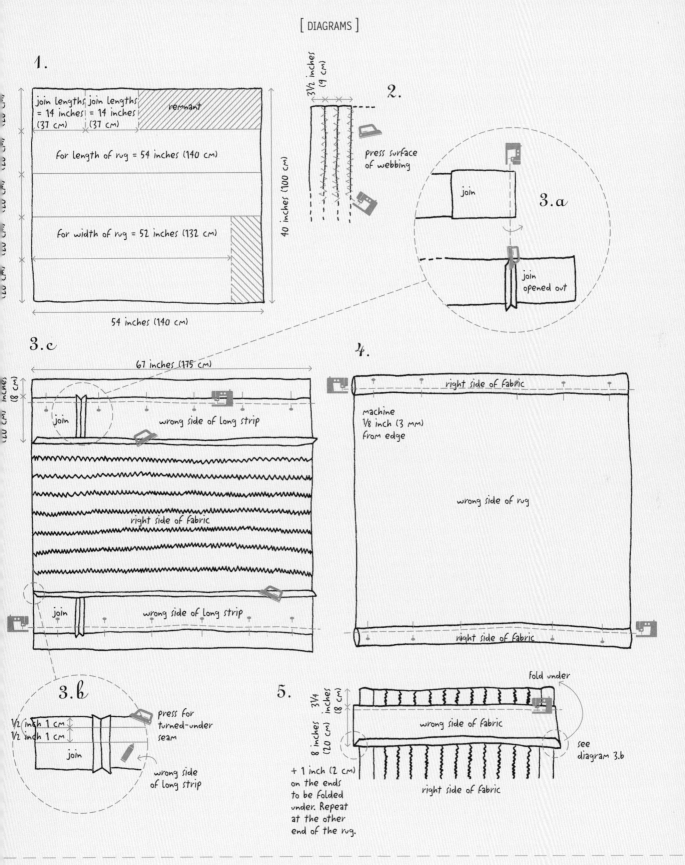

1.

join lengths = 14 inches (37 cm)
join lengths = 14 inches (37 cm)
remnant

for length of rug = 54 inches (140 cm)

for width of rug = 52 inches (132 cm)

40 inches (100 cm)

54 inches (140 cm)

2.

3½ inches (9 cm)

press surface of webbing

3.a

join

join opened out

3.c

67 inches (175 cm)

(8 cm)

join

wrong side of long strip

right side of fabric

join

wrong side of long strip

4.

right side of fabric

machine ⅛ inch (3 mm) from edge

wrong side of rug

right side of fabric

3.b

½ inch 1 cm
½ inch 1 cm

join

press for turned-under seam

wrong side of long strip

5.

3¼ inches (8 cm)

8 inches (20 cm)

+ 1 inch (2 cm) on the ends to be folded under. Repeat at the other end of the rug.

fold under

wrong side of fabric

see diagram 3.b

right side of fabric

Button-backed gallery chair

Do you collect buttons? Do you love them, hoard them, but really don't know what to do with them? Why not give free rein to your creative skills and use up all those odd buttons found in the flea markets (or antique stores) of Paris to create this chic chair back.

Shopping list

- MEDALLION CHAIR
- 1 RECTANGLE THICK COTTON FABRIC, 16 X 15 INCHES (40 X 38 CM)
- 1 RECTANGLE THICK IRON-ON INTERFACING, 16 X 15 INCHES (40 X 38 CM)
- 3 SHEETS PAPER, 11 X 17 INCHES
- SCOTCH TAPE
- LOTS OF BUTTONS (PREFERABLY MOTHER-OF-PEARL)

Sewing box

- PENCIL
- DRESSMAKING SCISSORS
- TAILOR'S CHALK
- FINE SEWING NEEDLE
- TAPE MEASURE OR RULER
- SPRAY TEXTILE ADHESIVE
- 3 SPOOLS WHITE PEARLIZED THREAD

1

Join the sheets of paper together with scotch tape. Position against the oval of the chair back and draw the outline to make a pattern [diagram 1.a]. Cut out the oval of the pattern, draw the outline onto the iron-on interfacing, and cut out [diagram 1.b].

2

Press the oval of iron-on interfacing onto the thick cotton fabric using a hot iron. Let cool and then cut out the fabric leaving a seam allowance of 1¼ inches (3 cm) around the iron-on oval [diagram 2.a]. Cut v-shaped notches around the edge of the fabric, press, fold down, and stick the notches to the iron-on interfacing with textile adhesive [diagram 2.b].

3

Cover the front of the oval with different sized buttons, overlapping them slightly, and stitching by hand with double pearlized thread [diagram 3.a]. Then stick the oval to the chair back with spray adhesive [diagram 3.b].

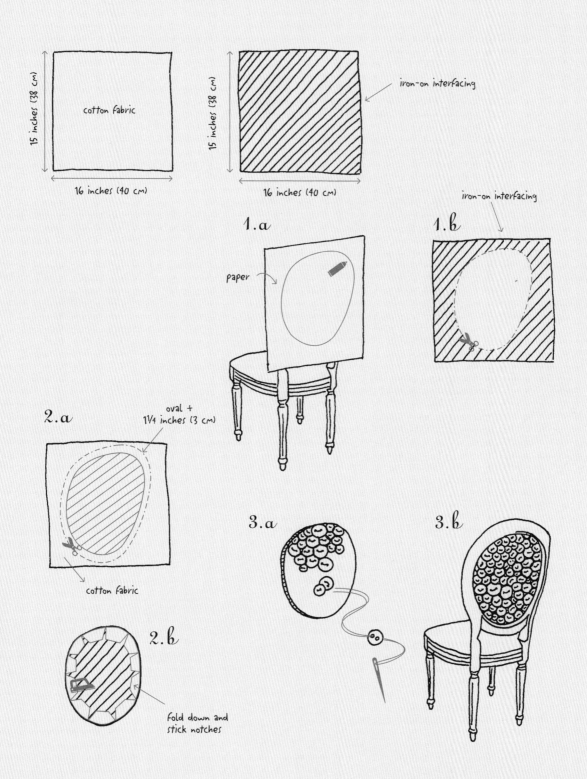

15 inches (38 cm)

cotton fabric

16 inches (40 cm)

15 inches (38 cm)

iron-on interfacing

16 inches (40 cm)

iron-on interfacing

1.a

paper

1.b

2.a

oval +
1¼ inches (3 cm)

cotton fabric

3.a

3.b

2.b

fold down and
stick notches

French cotton table runner

Shopping list

- 3/4 YARD (70 CM) COTTON DRAPERY FABRIC
  (LIGHT- OR MEDIUM-WEIGHT),
  54 OR 60 INCHES (140 OR 150 CM) WIDE

Sewing box

- TAILOR'S CHALK OR DRESSMAKER'S
  WHITE MARKING PENCIL
- PINS
- DRESSMAKING SCISSORS
- SEWING NEEDLE
- MATCHING THREAD

1

Measure the drop of your table cloth to determine the length of the table runner—54 or 60 inches (140 or 150 cm). The width will depend on the style of printed fabric you choose, around 18–22 inches (45–55 cm wide) [diagram 1.a]. Draw and cut out the rectangle of fabric, making sure you center the pattern on the runner. Machine double hems, 1/2 inch (1 cm) wide, on the long sides 1/12 inch (2 mm) from the edge [diagram 1.b].

2

Then machine non-mitered double hems, 1/2 inch (1 cm) wide, on the short sides, 1/12 inch (2 mm) from the edge.

Note

You can make mitered corners if you prefer.

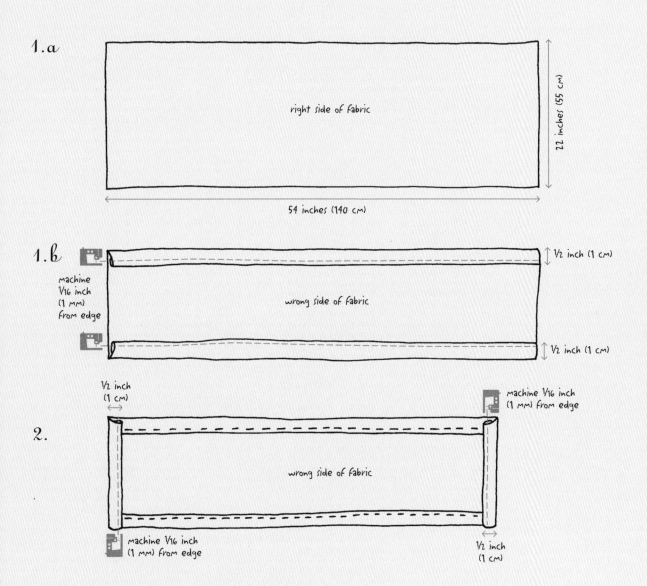

1.a

right side of fabric

22 inches (55 cm)

54 inches (140 cm)

1.b

machine
1/16 inch
(1 mm)
from edge

wrong side of fabric

1/2 inch (1 cm)

1/2 inch (1 cm)

2.

1/2 inch
(1 cm)

machine 1/16 inch
(1 mm) from edge

wrong side of fabric

machine 1/16 inch
(1 mm) from edge

1/2 inch
(1 cm)

Versailles velvet ottoman

Remember calculating the circumference of a circle in your math lessons? For this pattern us the formula 2 x 3.14 x radius = circumference, then add 1 inch (2 cm) for the seam allowance. You can vary the size of the ottoman to suit the size of the room or the space available.

Shopping list

- ¾ YARD (70 CM) STRIPED UPHOLSTERY FABRIC, 54 INCHES (140 CM) WIDE
- 1 PIECE HEAVYWEIGHT LINEN, 18 X 18 INCHES (45 X 45 CM)
- 1 SELF-COVER BUTTON, 1¼ INCHES (3 CM) IN DIAMETER
- 2 BAGS SHREDDED FOAM
- 1 2-LB (1-KG) BAG POLYESTER FIBERFILL

Sewing box

- TAILOR'S CHALK
- TAPE MEASURE
- PINS (DRESSMAKERS' AND ROUND-HEADED)
- DRESSMAKING SCISSORS
- MATCHING THREAD
- SEWING NEEDLE
- HEAVY-DUTY THREAD
- COMPASSES

1

Draw and cut out from the striped fabric a long strip—52 x 8½ inches (128 x 22 cm) and a square measuring 18 x 18 inches (45 x 45 cm). Using a compass, draw a 16-inch (40-cm) circle on each of the two square pieces of fabric. Cut out allowing an extra ½ inch (1 cm) for the seam.

2

Fold the long strip in half, right sides together and edge to edge, and machine ½ inch (1 cm) from the ends [diagram 2.a]. Mark the quarter circles with round-headed pins [diagram 2.b] or by making ¼-inch (5-mm) notches on the strip and the two circles.

3

Pin the striped circle and the side band of the ottoman, right sides together and edge to edge, taking care to match up the markers [diagram 3.a]. Machine ½ inch (1 cm) from the edge and then cut v-shaped notches around the edge of the seam [diagram 3.b]. Repeat with the linen circle, but only machine half way around the edge. Fold in and baste ½ inch (1 cm) on the other half. This large opening makes filling the ottoman much easier. Turn right side out.

4

Turn the cover upside down and stuff, starting with a layer of fiberfill over the base of the striped circle. Then fill the center generously with shredded foam, adding fiberfill around the edges to give a smooth finish [diagram 4.a]. Using the heavy-duty thread, close the opening by hand with running stitch. Cover the button with a scrap of the striped fabric (see page 34), and sew in the center of the top of the ottoman [diagram 4.b].

1.

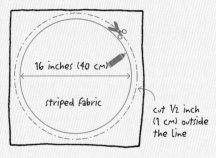

16 inches (40 cm)

striped fabric

cut ½ inch (1 cm) outside the line

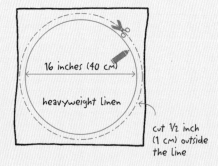

16 inches (40 cm)

heavyweight linen

cut ½ inch (1 cm) outside the line

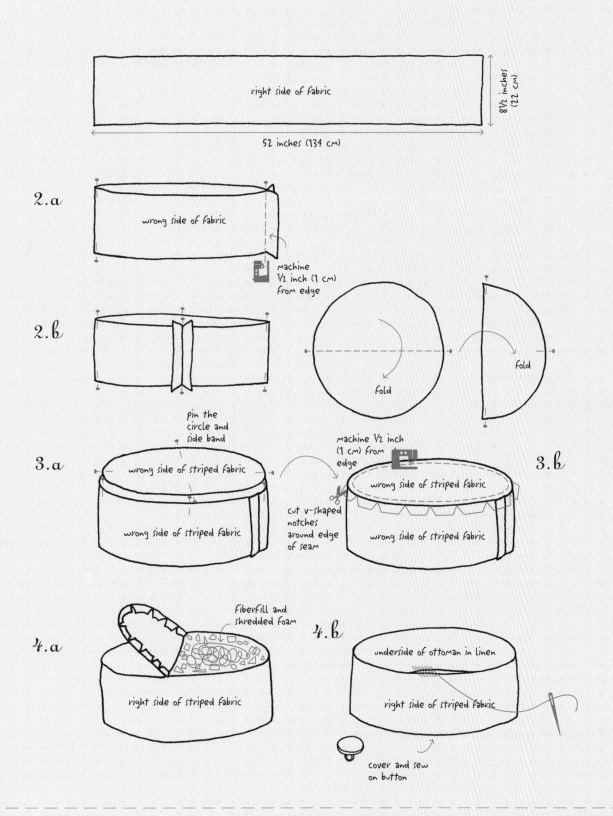

right side of fabric

8½ inches (22 cm)

52 inches (134 cm)

2.a

wrong side of fabric

machine ½ inch (1 cm) from edge

2.b

Fold

Fold

3.a

pin the circle and side band

wrong side of striped fabric

wrong side of striped fabric

cut v-shaped notches around edge of seam

machine ½ inch (1 cm) from edge

wrong side of striped fabric

wrong side of striped fabric

3.b

4.a

fiberfill and shredded foam

right side of striped fabric

4.b

underside of ottoman in linen

right side of striped fabric

cover and sew on button

Paris opera wrap

Shopping list

- 1½ YARDS (130 CM) PLAIN VELVET, 54 INCHES (140 CM) WIDE
- 1½ YARDS (130 CM) PLAIN VELVET (IN TONING SHADE), 54 INCHES (140 CM) WIDE
- 4 YARDS (3.6 M) WASHABLE POLYESTER BATTING, 54 INCHES (140 CM) WIDE
- 20 MOTHER-OF-PEARL BUTTONS (DIFFERENT SHAPES AND SIZES)

Sewing box

- TAILOR'S CHALK
- TAPE MEASURE
- PINS
- DRESSMAKING SCISSORS
- MATCHING THREAD
- SEWING NEEDLE
- HEAVY-DUTY THREAD

1

Cut out two rectangles of different colored velvet, each 54 x 48 inches (140 x 120 cm).

Cut out three rectangles of the polyester batting, each 53 x 47 inches (138 x 118 cm) [diagram 1.a]. Pin the rectangles for the cover, right sides together and edge to edge. Machine ½ inch (1 cm) from the edge in straight stitch, leaving a 24-inch (60-cm) opening. Trim off the corners ¹⁄₁₂ inch (2 mm) from the seam, then turn the cover right side out through the opening [diagram 1.b].

2

Machine the 3 layers of batting ½ inch (1 cm) from the edge using straight stitch [diagram 2.a]. Insert the batting into the cover and close the opening by hand using running stitch [diagram 2.b]. Handstitch the four corners and a few points around the edges of the wrap to hold the batting in place.

3

Sew the buttons on one side of the wrap, as shown.

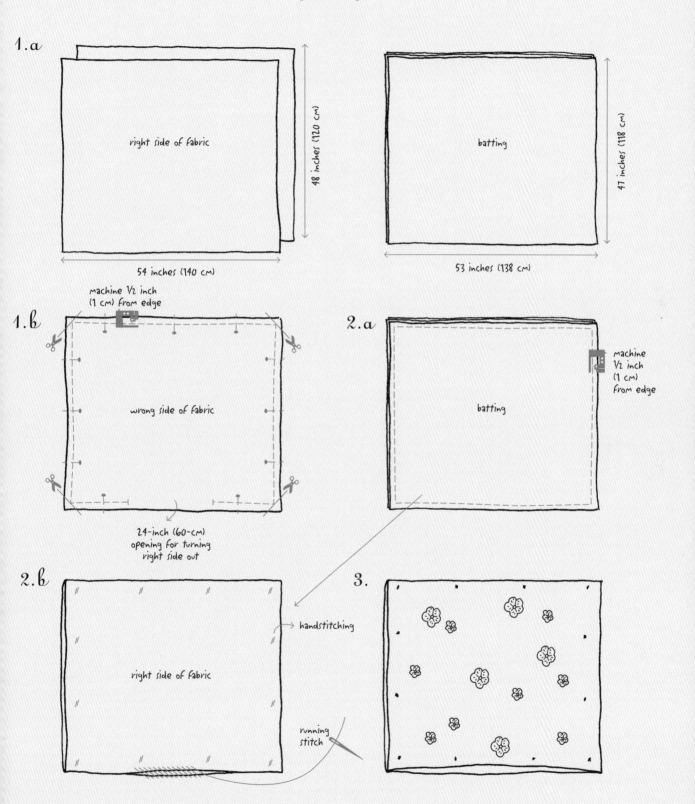

1.a

right side of fabric

48 inches (120 cm)

54 inches (140 cm)

batting

47 inches (118 cm)

53 inches (138 cm)

machine ½ inch
(1 cm) from edge

1.b

wrong side of fabric

24-inch (60-cm)
opening for turning
right side out

2.a

batting

machine
½ inch
(1 cm)
from edge

2.b

right side of fabric

handstitching

running
stitch

3.

Button-tufted cushion

Shopping list

- 1 PIECE VELVET FABRIC, AT LEAST
  17 X 17 INCHES (42 X 42 CM)
- 1 PIECE LINEN FABRIC (IN COMPLEMENTARY
  HUE), AT LEAST 17 X 17 INCHES
  (42 X 42 CM)
- SCRAP OF FABRIC FOR THE SELF-COVER
  BUTTONS
- 2 SELF-COVER BUTTONS, 1¼ INCHES
  (3 CM) IN DIAMETER
- 1 FEATHER-FILLED CUSHION PAD,
  16 X 16 INCHES (40 X 40 CM)

Sewing box

- TAILOR'S CHALK OR DRESSMAKER'S
  WHITE MARKING PENCIL
- RULER
- PINS
- DRESSMAKING SCISSORS
- MATCHING THREAD
- LONG SEWING NEEDLE
- THICK THREAD

1

Cut out squares from the two fabrics, each 17 x 17 inches (42 x 42 cm). Mark the center of each piece of fabric with the dressmaker's white marking pencil to indicate the position of the buttons.

2

Pin the squares, right sides together and edge to edge. Machine ½ inch (1 cm) from the edge in straight stitch, leaving an 8-inch (20-cm) opening on one side. Trim the corners ¹⁄₁₂ inch (2 mm) from the seam then turn the cushion cover right side out through the opening [diagram 2.a]. Press on the linen side. Insert the cushion pad inside the cover and close the opening by hand using running stitch [diagram 2.b].

3

Cover the two buttons (see page 34). Using the thick thread doubled, fasten the first button in position on one side of the cushion, then push the long needle through the center to the other side of the cushion, pulling the thread firmly so that the button sinks in. Thread the needle through the second button and push the needle back to the first side, again pulling the thread firmly. Wrap the thread around the first button to maintain the tension. Repeat the procedure few times, stitching through the shank of each button and finishing with a knot.

1.

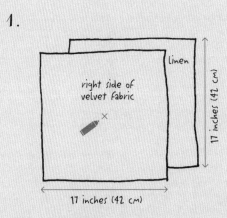

linen

right side of
velvet fabric

17 inches (42 cm)

17 inches (42 cm)

2.a

machine ½ inch
(1 cm) from edge

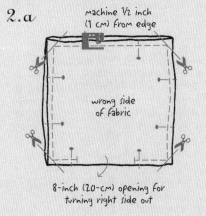

wrong side
of fabric

8-inch (20-cm) opening for
turning right side out

2.b

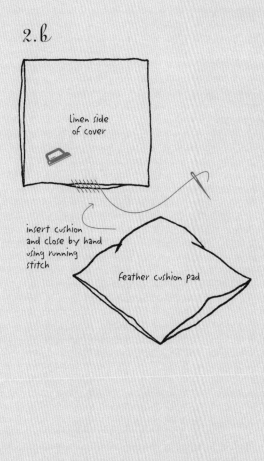

linen side
of cover

insert cushion
and close by hand
using running
stitch

feather cushion pad

3.

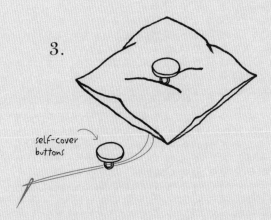

self-cover
buttons

Grommetted drapes

Before you start

Measure your window and adapt the measurements according to the size of the window and drape coverage desired. Allow an additional 2 inches (5 cm) to the length for the hem. If using a thick fabric, allow an extra 1 inch (2 cm) for turned-under hems.

Shopping list

- MEDIUM-WEIGHT DRAPERY FABRIC, 54 INCHES (140 CM) WIDE, LENGTH AS REQUIRED FOR EACH PANEL
- 1½ YARDS (140 CM) PER PANEL READY-TO-USE GROMMET TAPE (6 OR 8 GROMMETS PER YARD/METER)

Sewing box

- TAILOR'S CHALK OR DRESSMAKER'S WHITE MARKING PENCIL
- PINS
- DRESSMAKING SCISSORS
- SEWING NEEDLE
- MATCHING THREAD

1

Either leave the selvages visible or machine ½-inch (1-cm) double hems on the long sides of the panel, $\frac{1}{12}$ inch (2 mm) from the edge [diagram 1.a]. Then machine a non-mitered turned-under hem—2 inches (5 cm)—at the bottom of the panel [diagram 1.b].

2

Place the top of your panel onto the grommet tape, allowing at least an extra ½ inch (1 cm) on either side. Cut the grommet tape to the right length, turn the ends under ½ inch (1 cm), and baste [diagram 2.a]. Insert the fabric into the strip, pin, and baste [diagram 2.b]. Machine $\frac{1}{12}$ inch (2 mm) from the edge, starting with the short end of the grommet tape.

ready-to-use grommet tape

54 inches (140 cm)

fabric for one drape

54 inches (140 cm)

54 inches (140 cm)

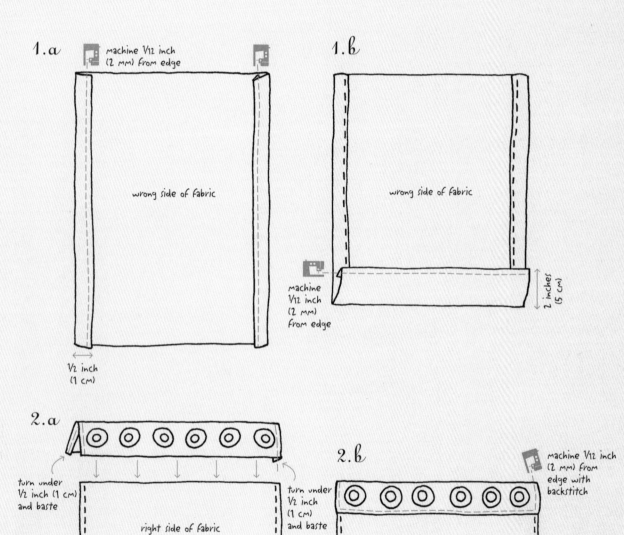

1.a

machine 1/12 inch (2 mm) from edge

wrong side of fabric

1/2 inch (1 cm)

1.b

wrong side of fabric

machine 1/12 inch (2 mm) from edge

2 inches (5 cm)

2.a

turn under 1/2 inch (1 cm) and baste

right side of fabric

turn under 1/2 inch (1 cm) and baste

2.b

machine 1/12 inch (2 mm) from edge with backstitch

right side of fabric

Warm and cozy

Baroque bolster cushi

[INSTRUCTIONS PAGE 98]

Cozy Provençal quilt

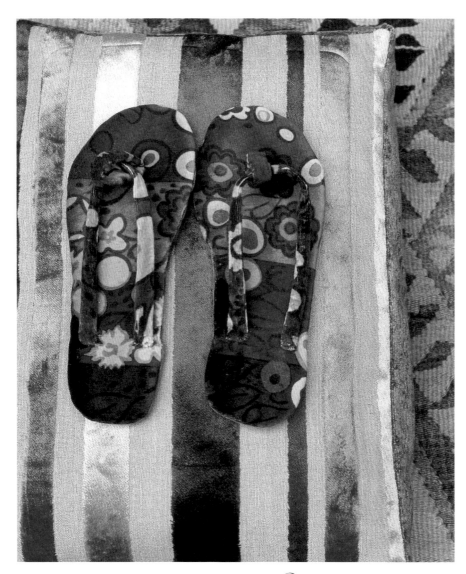

Bohemian flip flops

[INSTRUCTIONS PAGE 102]

Jacquard lampshade

[INSTRUCTIONS PAGE 106]

French deco chair

Tassel tie-back

Vivienne velvet cushions

Tassel tie-back

Shopping list

- 3/4 YARD (70 CM) THICK UPHOLSTERY FABRIC, 57 INCHES (144 CM) WIDE FOR ONE TIE-BACK, OR 1½ YARDS (140 CM) FOR A PAIR

Sewing box

- TAILOR'S CHALK OR DRESSMAKER'S WHITE MARKING PENCIL
- PINS
- DRESSMAKING SCISSORS
- SEWING NEEDLE
- MATCHING THREAD
- MEDIUM-SIZED CROCHET HOOK

Before you start

Choose a thick, loosely woven fabric which is easy to unravel.

1

Cut out two strips for the cords—one 2 x 28½ inches (5 x 72 cm) and one 2 x 57 inches (5 x 144 cm). Then cut out two rectangles 23 x 28½ inches (57 x 72 cm) for the tassels.

2

To make the tassels, cut off the selvages and, using a crochet hook, unravel the threads for 12 inches (30 cm) on one of the long sides of both rectangles of fabric, working from the center toward the edge.

3

Mark the side edges of the fabric at 3½-inch (9-cm) intervals and draw lines to indicate the folds of the turndowns. Turn in ½ inch (1 cm) along one of the edges, pin, and baste [diagram 3.a]. Fold, pin, and baste the two 3½-inch (9-cm) turndowns [diagram 3.b]. Repeat for the second piece of fabric.

4

To make the cords, turn in and press ½ inch (1 cm) along both sides, then fold in half lengthwise and handstitch with running stitch [diagram 4.a]. Make a "hangman's knot" (see diagram page 247) with the longer of the two cords, leaving 5-inch (13-cm) ends.

Measure the loop and cut the other cord to make a loop the same size as the first, allowing an extra 1 inch (2 cm) at each end [diagram 4.b]. Sew the ends, insert into the "hangman's knot," and handstitch to secure.

5

Handstitch 1 inch (2 cm) of one of the cord ends to the unhemmed edge of the unraveled fabric. Roll the fabric tightly round the cord and secure by hand with running stitch. Remove any visible basting. Repeat with the second piece of unraveled fabric.

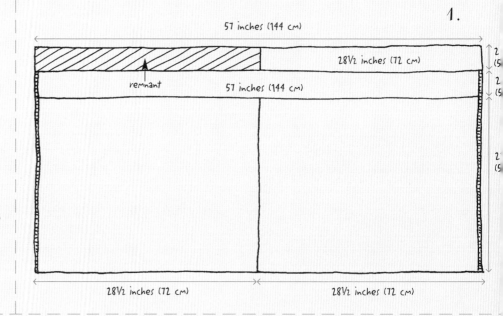

1.

57 inches (144 cm)

28½ inches (72 cm)

remnant

57 inches (144 cm)

28½ inches (72 cm)

28½ inches (72 cm)

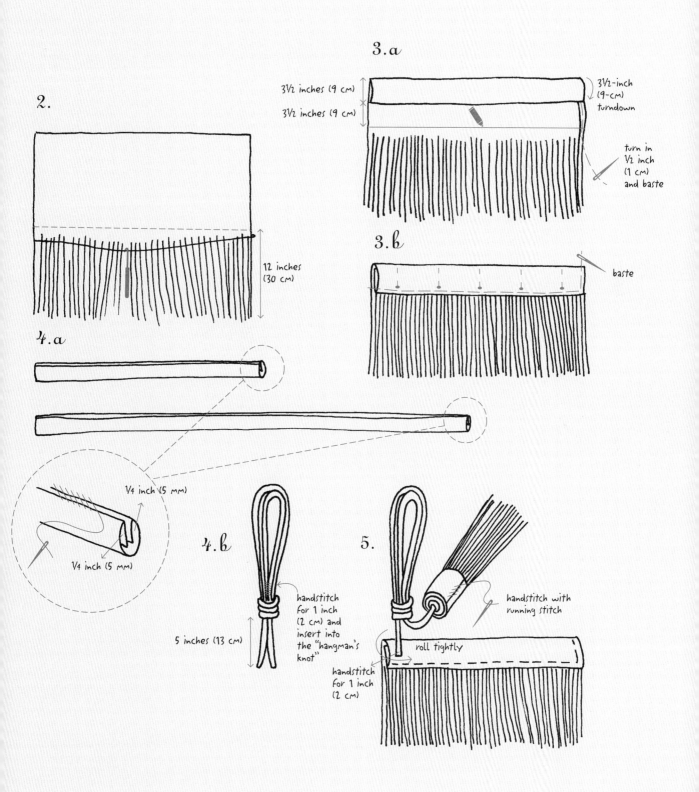

2.

12 inches (30 CM)

3.a

3½ inches (9 CM)

3½ inches (9 CM)

3½-inch (9-CM) turndown

turn in ½ inch (1 CM) and baste

3.b

baste

4.a

¼ inch (5 MM)

¼ inch (5 MM)

4.b

5 inches (13 CM)

handstitch for 1 inch (2 CM) and insert into the "hangman's knot"

handstitch for 1 inch (2 CM)

5.

handstitch with running stitch

roll tightly

Cozy Provençal quilt

Shopping list

- 1⅓ yards (120 cm) patterned velvet, 54 inches (140 cm) wide
- 1⅓ yards (120 cm) plain, contrasting velvet, 54 inches (140 cm) wide
- 4 yards (3.6 m) washable polyester batting, 54 inches (140 cm) wide

Sewing box

- tailor's chalk
- tape measure
- pins
- dressmaking scissors
- matching thread
- sewing needle

1

Cut out a rectangle 54 x 48 inches (140 x 120 cm) from each of the two velvet fabrics and three rectangles 53 x 47 inches (138 x 118 cm) from the batting [diagram 1.a]. Pin the fabric right sides together and edge to edge. Machine ½ inch (1 cm) from the edge in straight stitch, leaving a 24-inch (60-cm) opening. Cut off the corners $\frac{1}{12}$ inch (2 mm) from the seam, then turn the cover right side out through the opening [diagram 1.b].

2

Put the three rectangles of batting together and machine ½ inch (1 cm) from the edge in straight stitch [diagram 2.a]. Insert the layers of batting into the cover. Close the opening by hand using running stitch. Handstitch the four corners and a few points around the edges of the quilt to hold the felting in place [diagram 2.b].

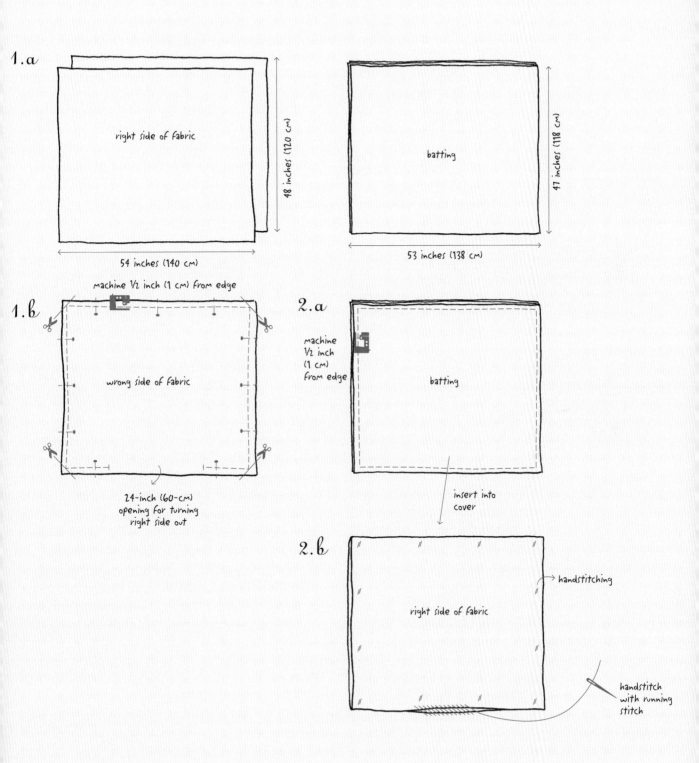

1.a

right side of fabric

48 inches (120 cm)

54 inches (140 cm)

batting

47 inches (118 cm)

53 inches (138 cm)

machine ½ inch (1 cm) from edge

1.b

wrong side of fabric

24-inch (60-cm) opening for turning right side out

2.a

machine ½ inch (1 cm) from edge

batting

insert into cover

2.b

handstitching

right side of fabric

handstitch with running stitch

Baroque bolster cushion

Shopping list

- ³/4 YARD (70 CM) VELVET JACQUARD FABRIC, 40 INCHES (100 CM) WIDE
- ³/4 YARD (70 CM) COTTON FABRIC, 40 INCHES (100 CM) WIDE
- 3 FEATHER PILLOWS, FOR THE STUFFING (OR USE POLYESTER FIBERFILL)

Sewing box

- TAILOR'S CHALK OR DRESSMAKER'S WHITE MARKING PENCIL
- PINS
- DRESSMAKING SCISSORS
- SEWING NEEDLE
- MATCHING THREAD

1

Cut out a rectangle 25 x 40 inches (62 x 100 cm) from the velvet jacquard fabric taking care to center the motif. Fold the rectangle in half lengthwise and pin right sides together and edge to edge.

2

Machine ½ inch (1 cm) from the edge, leaving a 10-inch (25-cm) opening in the center.

3

Open out the seam and press flat. Position the pressed seam in the center of the rectangle. Pin the two ends and machine ½ inch (1 cm) from the edge. Cut off the corners and turn the cover right side out through the opening. Repeat steps 1–3 for the cotton cover and stuff with the feathers. Close the opening by hand using running stitch.

4

Insert the feather-filled cushion into the patterned cover and close the opening by hand using running stitch.

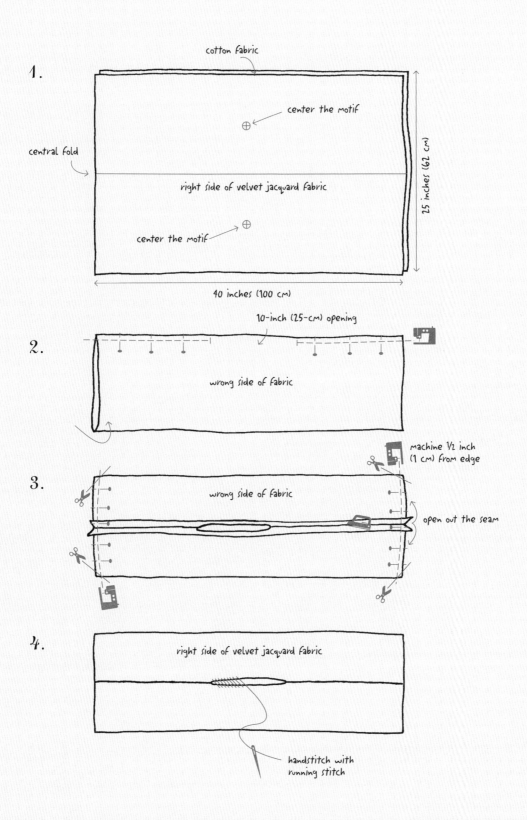

1.

cotton fabric

center the motif

central fold

right side of velvet jacquard fabric

25 inches (62 cm)

center the motif

40 inches (100 cm)

2.

10-inch (25-cm) opening

wrong side of fabric

3.

machine ½ inch (1 cm) from edge

wrong side of fabric

open out the seam

4.

right side of velvet jacquard fabric

handstitch with running stitch

Vivienne velvet cushions

Shopping list

- REMNANT OF STRIPED VELVET FABRIC, AT LEAST 18½ X 14 INCHES (47 X 35 CM)
- REMNANT OF PLAIN VELVET FABRIC, AT LEAST 25½ X 21 INCHES (65 X 53 CM)
- REMNANT OF COTTON FABRIC, AT LEAST 35 X 22 INCHES (88 X 56 CM)
- 2 FEATHER PILLOWS, FOR STUFFING (OR USE POLYESTER FIBERFILL)

Sewing box

- TAILOR'S CHALK OR DRESSMAKER'S WHITE MARKING PENCIL
- PINS
- DRESSMAKING SCISSORS
- SEWING NEEDLE
- MATCHING THREAD

1

From the striped velvet fabric, cut out one rectangle 14 x 18½ inches (35 x 47 cm). From the plain velvet fabric, cut out one rectangle 14 x 18½ inches (35 x 47 cm), two strips 3½ x 14 inches (9 x 35 cm), and two strips 3½ x 18½ inches (9 x 47 cm).

From the cotton fabric, cut out two rectangles 14 x 18½ inches (35 x 47 cm), two strips 3½ x 14 inches (9 x 35 cm), and two strips 3½ x 18½ inches (9 x 47 cm).

2

Pin the four strips of plain velvet, right sides together and edge to edge, alternating the longer and shorter pieces. Join to form a rectangle. Machine ½ inch (1 cm) from the edge.

3

Pin the striped fabric to the strips forming the edges, right sides together and edge to edge. Machine ½ inch (1 cm) from the edge.

4

Pin the plain velvet fabric rectangle (back of the cushion), right sides together and edge to edge, to the rest of the cushion cover. Machine ½ inch (1 cm) from the edge, leaving a 12-inch (30-cm) opening. Turn the cover right side out through the opening. Repeat steps 1–4 for the cotton cover and fill with feathers. Close the opening by hand using running stitch.

5

Insert the feather-filled cushion into the cover and close the opening by hand using running stitch.

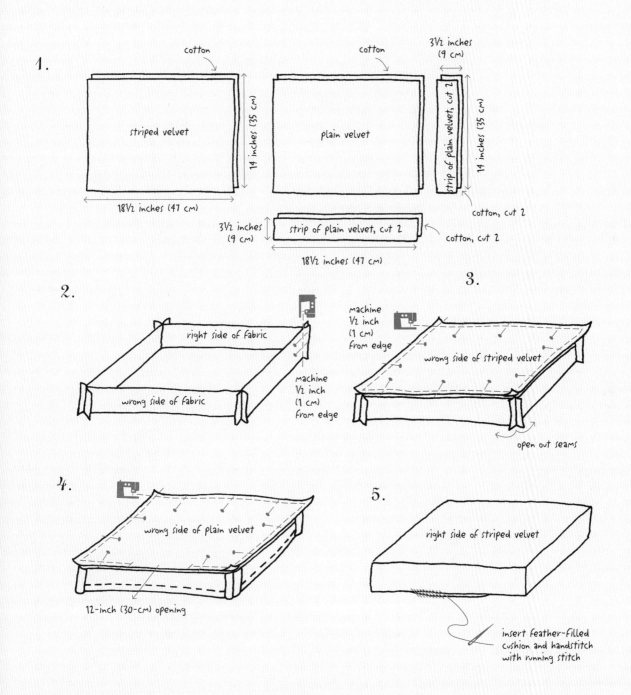

1.

cotton

striped velvet

14 inches (35 cm)

18½ inches (47 cm)

cotton

plain velvet

3½ inches (9 cm)

strip of plain velvet, cut 2

14 inches (35 cm)

cotton, cut 2

3½ inches (9 cm)

strip of plain velvet, cut 2

cotton, cut 2

18½ inches (47 cm)

2.

right side of fabric

wrong side of fabric

machine ½ inch (1 cm) from edge

3.

machine ½ inch (1 cm) from edge

wrong side of striped velvet

open out seams

4.

wrong side of plain velvet

12-inch (30-cm) opening

5.

right side of striped velvet

insert feather-filled cushion and handstitch with running stitch

Bohemian flip flops

Shopping list

- REMNANT OF PATTERNED VELVET FABRIC
  12 x 18 INCHES (30 x 46 CM)
- REMNANT OF PLAIN VELVET FABRIC
  12 x 12 INCHES (30 x 30 CM)
- REMNANT OF COTTON BATTING
  12 x 36 INCHES (30 x 90 CM)

Sewing box

- TAILOR'S CHALK OR DRESSMAKER'S
  WHITE MARKING PENCIL
- PINS
- DRESSMAKING SCISSORS
- SEWING NEEDLE
- MATCHING THREAD
- WOODEN STICK (USE A FINE PAINTBRUSH
  OR CHOPSTICK), OR KNITTING NEEDLE

before you start

Make a pattern by drawing around an old pair of flip flops, or photocopy the pattern on page 250, enlarging it accordingly.

1

Cut out the pattern. Then cut out the following rectangles: two pieces 6 x 12 inches (15 x 30 cm), two pieces 2 x 12 inches (5 x 30 cm), and two pieces 2 x 5½ inches (5 x 14 cm) from the printed velvet fabric; two pieces 6 x 12 inches (15 x 30 cm) from the plain velvet fabric; and six pieces 6 x 12 inches (15 x 30 cm) from the cotton batting.

2

Pin the 6 x 12-inch (15 x 30-cm) pairs of rectangles of patterned and plain velvet right sides together and edge to edge. Draw the pattern onto the fabric, remembering to reverse it for the opposite foot. Cut out the various pieces ½ inch (1 cm) outside the line to allow for the seams [diagram 2.a]. For the three layers of cotton batting, cut ⅛ inch (3 mm) inside the line [diagram 2.b].

3

Machine the three layers of cotton batting ¼ inch (5 mm) from the edge and then machine two seams running the length of the sole to hold the layers in place.

4

Pin the patterned and plain velvet soles right sides together and edge to edge. Machine ½ inch (1 cm) from the edge (i.e. on the outline of the pattern), leaving an opening on the outside edge [diagram 4.a]. Turn right side out and insert the padded sole. Close the opening by hand using running stitch [diagram 4.b].

5

Fold the two narrow rectangles (straps) in half lengthwise, right sides together, and machine ½ inch (1 cm) from the edge [diagram 5.a]. Trim ¼ inch (5 mm) off the seam. Using a wooden stick or knitting needle, turn the straps right side out, then turn in ½ inch (1 cm) at the open ends and stitch [diagram 5.b].

6

Fold the smaller strap in half and handstitch the ends to form a loop. Thread the longer strap through the loop and handstitch both parts of the strap to the sole with running stitch (see markers on pattern, page 250). Repeat for the other flip flop.

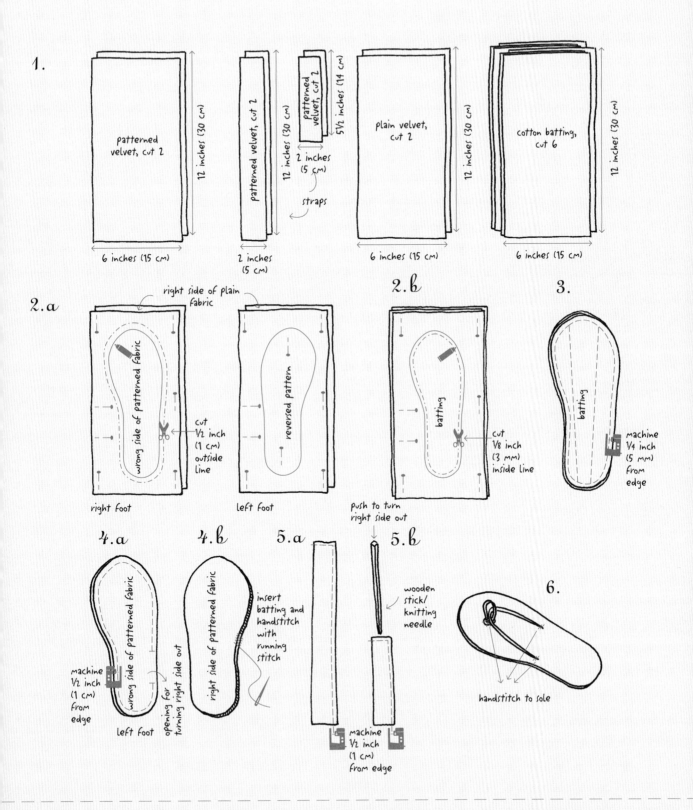

1.

patterned velvet, cut 2
12 inches (30 cm)
6 inches (15 cm)

patterned velvet, cut 2
12 inches (30 cm)
2 inches (5 cm)

patterned velvet, cut 2
5½ inches (14 cm)
2 inches (5 cm)
straps

plain velvet, cut 2
12 inches (30 cm)
6 inches (15 cm)

cotton batting, cut 6
12 inches (30 cm)
6 inches (15 cm)

2.a
right side of plain fabric
wrong side of patterned fabric
cut ½ inch (1 cm) outside line
right foot

reversed pattern
left foot

2.b
batting
cut ⅛ inch (3 mm) inside line
push to turn right side out

3.
batting
machine ¼ inch (5 mm) from edge

4.a
wrong side of patterned fabric
machine ½ inch (1 cm) from edge
opening for turning right side out
left foot

4.b
right side of patterned fabric
insert batting and handstitch with running stitch

5.a
machine ½ inch (1 cm) from edge

5.b
wooden stick/ knitting needle

6.
handstitch to sole

French deco chair

- 1¼ YARDS (1 M) STRIPED VELVET FABRIC, 54 INCHES (140 CM) WIDE
- HIGH-BACKED UPHOLSTERED CHAIR

Sewing box

- TAILOR'S CHALK OR DRESSMAKER'S WHITE MARKING PENCIL
- PINS
- DRESSMAKING SCISSORS
- LONG, STRONG UPHOLSTERY NEEDLE
- PLIERS
- HEAVY-DUTY MATCHING THREAD

1

Measure the seat of the chair and cut a rectangle out of the fabric 2 inches (5 cm) larger than the seat.

2

Position the fabric on the surface of the seat, taking care to center the stripes and allowing an extra 2 inches (5 cm) at the back. Draw the outline of the seat on the wrong side of the fabric, [diagram 2.a], then place it flat and cut 1 inch (2 cm) outside the line [diagram 2.b]. Cut v-shaped notches every 2 inches (5 cm) [diagram 2.c].

3

Place the cut fabric on the seat. Push the 2-inch (5-cm) border of fabric firmly (with a strong ruler, for example) into the gap between the seat and the chair back. Fold the notches under the striped fabric and secure it with pins.

4

Thread the needle with heavy-duty thread, pull the thread through so that the strand is doubled and knot the ends. Handstitch the striped fabric to the chair with running stitch every ⅝ inch (1.5 cm), sewing through the piping and using the pliers to help pull the needle, if necessary.

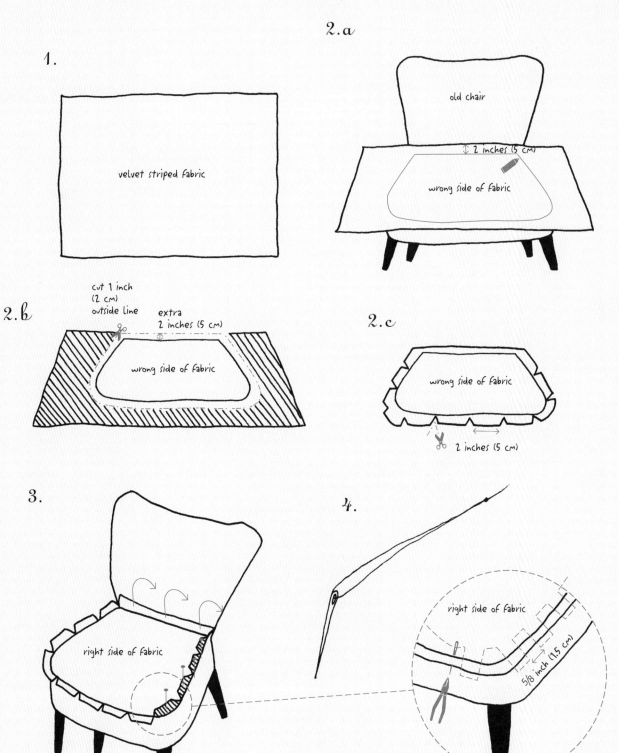

2.a

1.

velvet striped fabric

old chair

‡ 2 inches (5 cm)

wrong side of fabric

2.b

cut 1 inch
(2 cm)
outside line

extra
2 inches (5 cm)

wrong side of fabric

2.c

wrong side of fabric

2 inches (5 cm)

3.

right side of fabric

4.

right side of fabric

5/8 inch (1.5 cm)

Jacquard lampshade

Shopping list

- 1 RECTANGLE OF VELVET JACQUARD FABRIC, THE SAME SIZE AS YOUR LAMPSHADE PLUS SEAM ALLOWANCES
- 1 SQUARE LAMPSHADE

Sewing box

- DRESSMAKING SCISSORS
- TAPE MEASURE
- RULER
- TAILOR'S CHALK
- MATCHING THREAD
- PINS

1

Measure your lampshade with the tape measure and add 1¼ inches (3 cm) to the height and 1 inch (2 cm) to the length [diagram 1].

2

Taking account of the position of the motif, and making sure the seam coincides with one of the ribs [diagram 2.a] at the back of the lampshade, draw and cut out the rectangle of fabric [diagram 2.b].

3

On the long sides, draw the lines that mark the folds for the single ½-inch (1-cm) hems. Press to mark the single hems [diagram 3.a], then unfold. With right sides together and edge to edge, pin the ends of the fabric ½ inch (1 cm) from the edge. Machine in straight stitch [diagram 3.b] and then open out the seam.

4

Turn down the two pressed single hems and machine in straight stitch ¹⁄₁₆ inch (1 mm) from the edge. Turn the cover right side out and place over the lampshade.

Note

If you have chosen a fairly fine fabric, sew double hems at the top and bottom—add 2 inches (5 cm) to the height [diagram 1] and machine ¹⁄₁₂ inch (2 mm) from the edge). When placing the cover over the lampshade, stretch the fabric so that the shade doesn't wrinkle. You don't need to stretch medium- and heavyweight fabrics.

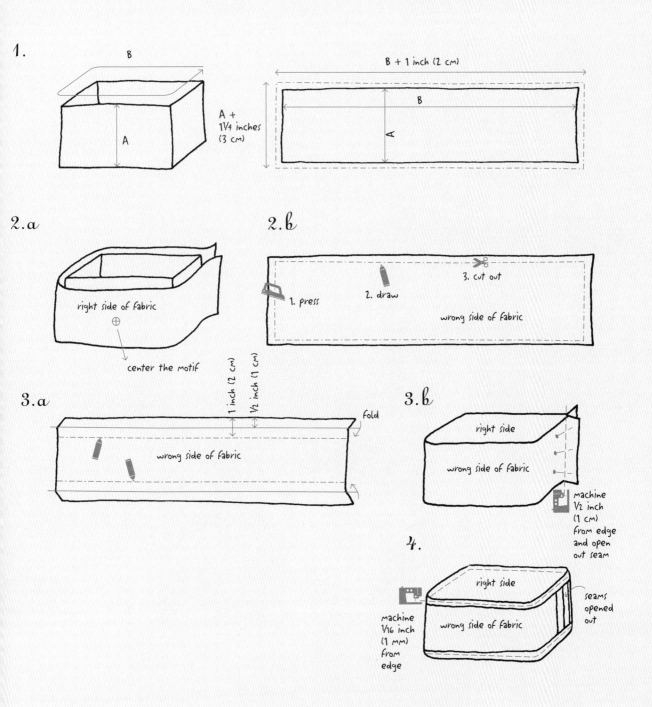

1.

B

A

B + 1 inch (2 cm)

B

A

A +
1¼ inches
(3 cm)

2.a

right side of fabric

center the motif

2.b

1. press

2. draw

3. cut out

wrong side of fabric

3.a

1 inch (2 cm)

½ inch (1 cm)

fold

wrong side of fabric

3.b

right side

wrong side of fabric

machine
½ inch
(1 cm)
from edge
and open
out seam

4.

machine
1/16 inch
(1 mm)
from
edge

right side

wrong side of fabric

seams
opened
out

Kitchen essentials

French chef's apron

Bourgeois bag organizer

Café blinds

Bistro place mat

[INSTRUCTIONS PAGE 120]

Brasserie tablecloth

[INSTRUCTIONS PAGE 126]

Giverny flowered chair

Saturday market caddy

Café blinds

Contemporary fabric designers offer some truly amazing motifs, colors, and fabrics. So why not indulge yourself? Just a basic café towel, combined with a yard of fabric, are enough to make several distinctively French accessories.

Shopping list

- DISH TOWEL TO FIT THE WIDTH OF YOUR WINDOW
- 1 YARD (90 CM) OF FABRIC WITH A KITCHEN MOTIF
- 2 BRASS CURTAIN RODS

Sewing box

- TAPE MEASURE
- PINS
- MATCHING THREAD
- NEEDLE

1

Fix the brass curtain rods above the window [diagram 1.a]. Take measurements A and B for the blinds and add an allowance for hems—½ inch (1 cm) per side for the ¼-inch (5-mm) double hems, ½ inch (1 cm) for each of the French seams (see page 27), and 1 inch (2 cm) for the top [diagram 1.b]. Cut out the different pieces of the panel based on these measurements, adjusting your pieces of fabric depending on the motif.

2

Join the pieces using French seams [diagram 2.a], and sew the top two pieces of the blind ½ inch (1 cm) from the edge, with the wrong side of the dish towel against the right side of the patterned fabric [diagram 2.b].

3

Sew the ¼-inch (5-mm) double hems on the sides [diagram 3.a]. Fold and press a ½-inch (1-cm) fold at the top of the blind. To make the hem and casing for the brass curtain rod, fold the top edge down over the right side of the drape and topstitch 1/12 inch (2 mm) from the top and bottom edges of this hem [diagram 3.b]. For the casing, machine a line of topstitching 1½ inches (4 cm) from the bottom edge of the hem. Make the other blind to match.

1.a

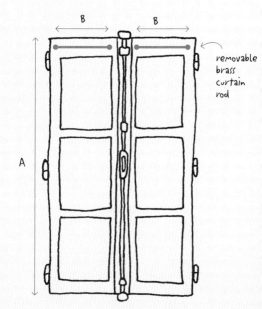

removable brass curtain rod

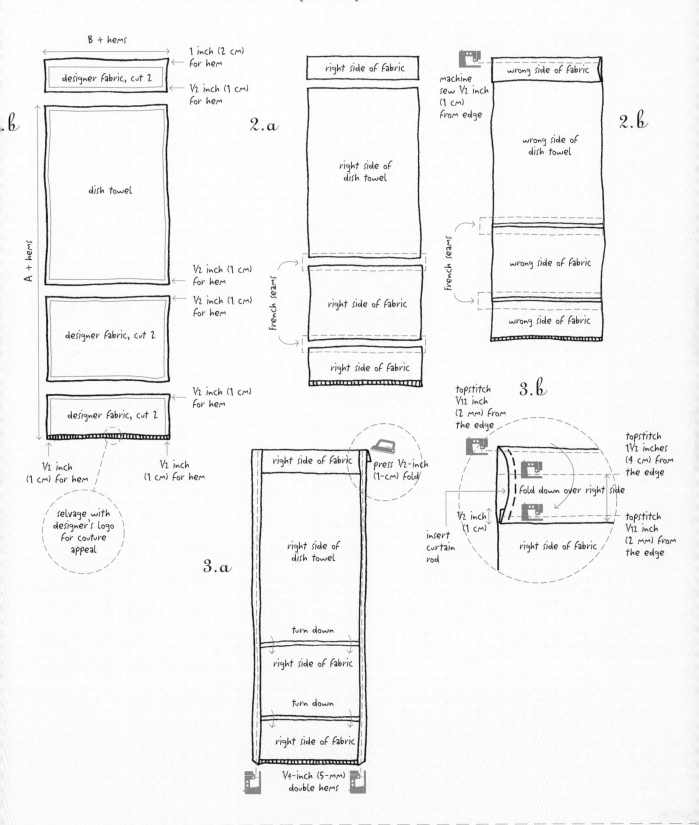

B + hems

1 inch (2 cm) for hem

designer fabric, cut 2

½ inch (1 cm) for hem

.b

A + hems

dish towel

½ inch (1 cm) for hem

½ inch (1 cm) for hem

designer fabric, cut 2

½ inch (1 cm) for hem

designer fabric, cut 2

½ inch (1 cm) for hem

½ inch (1 cm) for hem

selvage with designer's logo for couture appeal

2.a

right side of Fabric

right side of dish towel

French seams

½ inch (1 cm) for hem

right side of Fabric

right side of Fabric

2.b

machine sew ½ inch (1 cm) from edge

wrong side of Fabric

wrong side of dish towel

French seams

wrong side of fabric

wrong side of fabric

3.a

right side of Fabric

press ½-inch (1-cm) fold

right side of dish towel

turn down

right side of Fabric

turn down

right side of Fabric

¼-inch (5-mm) double hems

3.b

topstitch 1/12 inch (2 mm) from the edge

topstitch 1½ inches (4 cm) from the edge

Fold down over right side

insert curtain rod

½ inch (1 cm)

topstitch 1/12 inch (2 mm) from the edge

right side of Fabric

Bistro place mat

Facile fabriquer! The easiest accessory you can make, sans fuss.

Shopping list

- 1 DISH TOWEL 20 X 28 INCHES
  (50 X 70 CM)
- 1 MOTIF FROM A REMNANT OF COTTON
  FABRIC (E.G. A CUP)

Sewing box

- TAILOR'S CHALK
- RULER
- PINS
- DRESSMAKING SCISSORS
- MATCHING THREAD

1

Cut out the motif allowing an extra
5/8 inch (1.5 cm) around the outline.
Cut v-shaped notches around the
outline, fold down and press on the
wrong side of the fabric [diagram 1.a].
Pin the motif on one half of the dish
towel. Machine in straight stitch
1/16 inch (1 mm) from the edge of
the motif [diagram 1.b].

2

Fold the dish towel in half, right
sides facing, and pin edge to edge.
Machine the three sides in straight
stitch ½ inch (1 cm) from the edge.
Leave an opening of 6 inches (15 cm).
Cut off the corners.

3

Turn right side out through the
opening. Press the surface to flatten
the seams and topstitch ¹⁄₁₂ inch
(2 mm) from the edge on all four
sides of the place mat.

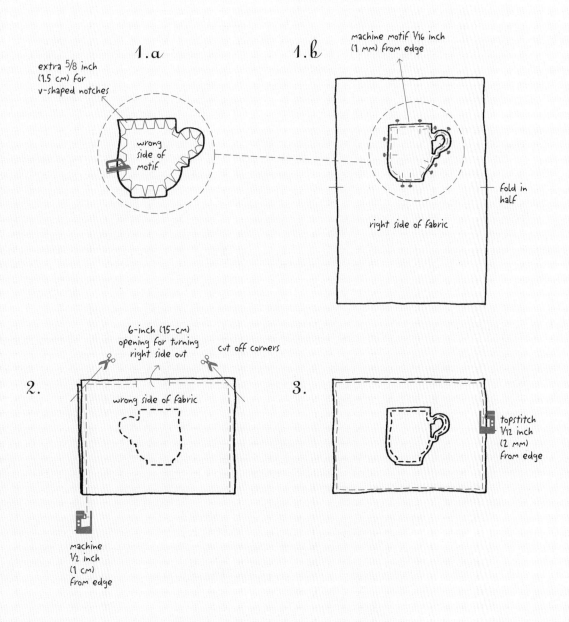

1.a

extra 5/8 inch (1.5 cm) for v-shaped notches

wrong side of motif

1.b

machine motif 1/16 inch (1 mm) from edge

fold in half

right side of fabric

2.

6-inch (15-cm) opening for turning right side out

cut off corners

wrong side of fabric

machine 1/2 inch (1 cm) from edge

3.

topstitch 1/12 inch (2 mm) from edge

Bourgeois bag organizer

A dish towel, a little bit of magic, and voila! you've got a bag organizer!

Shopping list

- 1 DISH TOWEL 20 X 28 INCHES (50 X 70 CM)
- 1 YARD (1 M) RED SYNTHETIC WEBBING, 1¼ INCHES (3 CM) WIDE

Sewing box

- TAILOR'S CHALK
- RULER
- PINS
- DRESSMAKING SCISSORS
- MATCHING THREAD

1

Fold down and press a 3½-inch (9-cm) hem along one of the long sides of the dish towel. Topstitch the top of the fold ¼ inch (5 mm) from the edge.

2

Cut out two 20-inch (50-cm) lengths from the webbing. Melt the ends carefully with a cigarette lighter to stop them fraying. Position and pin the handles in place [diagram 2.a]. Machine the handles in straight stitch, sewing a rectangle ¹⁄₁₆ inch (1 mm) from the edge and then a central cross [diagram 2.b].

3

Fold the dish towel in half, right sides facing, and pin edge to edge. Machine the two sides ½ inch (1 cm) from the edge in straight stitch, leaving an opening of 6 inches (15 cm) for removing the plastic bags.

4

Make folded corners on the sides of the bag by machining a seam 4 inches (10 cm) from the corner. Fold the corners upward and handstitch to secure. Turn right side out through the opening at the top.

1.

topstitch
¼ inch
(5 mm)
from edge

right side of dish towel

3½-inch
(9-cm)
Fold

2.b handles

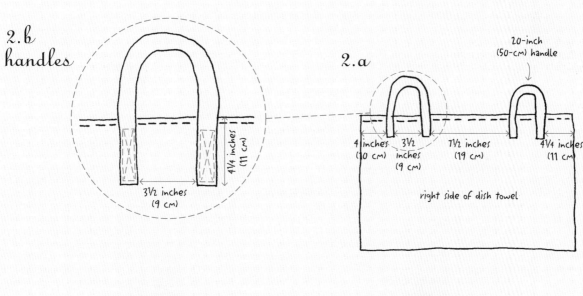

4¼ inches
(11 cm)

3½ inches
(9 cm)

2.a

20-inch
(50-cm) handle

4 inches
(10 cm)

3½
inches
(9 cm)

7½ inches
(19 cm)

4¼ inches
(11 cm)

right side of dish towel

3.

wrong side of fabric

machine
½ inch
(1 cm)
from edge

6-inch (15-cm)
opening for pulling
out bags

4.

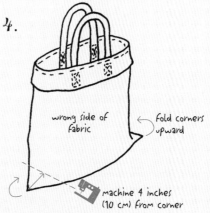

wrong side of
fabric

Fold corners
upward

machine 4 inches
(10 cm) from corner

Giverny flowered chair

"Sewn" with a staple gun.

Shopping list

- SECONDHAND CHAIR WITH A SEAT THAT CAN BE UNSCREWED FROM UNDERNEATH
- REMNANT OF OILCLOTH 24 X 24 INCHES (60 X 60 CM), DEPENDING ON THE SIZE OF THE SEAT
- REMNANT OF LINEN 20 X 20 INCHES (50 X 50 CM), DEPENDING ON THE SIZE OF THE SEAT
- SHEET OF FOAM PADDING, DEPENDING ON THE STATE OF THE ORIGINAL AND SIZE OF THE SEAT
- STAPLE GUN

Sewing box

- PENCIL
- TWO RULERS
- DRESSMAKING SCISSORS

Before you start

Unscrew the seat and clean the chair. Remove the staples from the old fabric of the seat with a small screwdriver. Depending on its condition, change the foam padding. Keep the fabric from the top and underside of the seat to use as templates for the patterns.

1

Using the fabric from the top of the seat as a template, place it against the wrong side of the oilcloth and cut out the shape. If the fabric is unusable, place the seat itself upside down on the wrong side of the oilcloth and, using two rulers, draw an outline parallel to the sides of the seat on the oilcloth.

2

Depending on the thickness (base and foam), leave a border of 2–2³/4 inches (5–7 cm) around the outline for folding under the seat. Cut out.

3

Fold the first two opposite sides under the seat and staple every 1¹/4 inches (3 cm) [diagram 3.a]. Then pull and tuck the oilcloth to form neat corners by folding down the other two opposite sides. Staple as before [diagram 3.b].

4

Draw the pattern for the underside of the seat on the linen, marking the holes for the screws. Press a single 1-inch (2-cm) hem around the edge, then staple the linen to the underside of the seat. Screw the seat onto the chair.

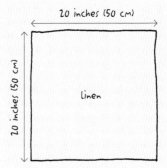

20 inches (50 cm)

20 inches (50 cm)

linen

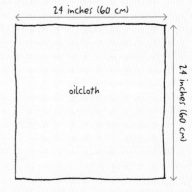

24 inches (60 cm)

24 inches (60 cm)

oilcloth

1.

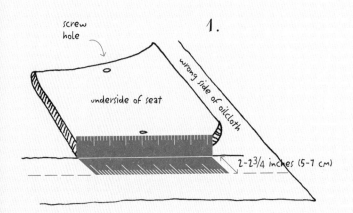

screw hole

underside of seat

wrong side of oilcloth

2-2³/4 inches (5-7 cm)

2.

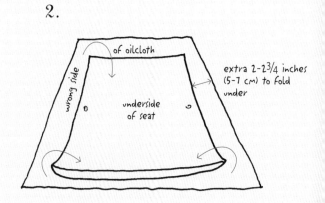

of oilcloth

wrong side

underside of seat

extra 2-2³/4 inches (5-7 cm) to fold under

3.a

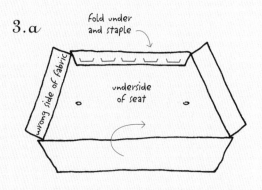

fold under and staple

underside of seat

wrong side of fabric

3.b

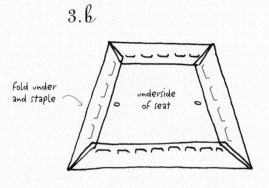

fold under and staple

underside of seat

4.

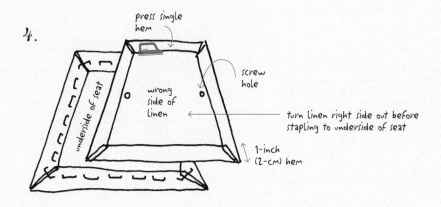

press single hem

screw hole

underside of seat

wrong side of linen

turn linen right side out before stapling to underside of seat

1-inch (2-cm) hem

Brasserie tablecloth

Leave the china to dry by itself. . .

Shopping list
- 6 DISH TOWELS 20 X 28 INCHES (50 X 70 CM)

Sewing box
- TAILOR'S CHALK
- RULER
- PINS
- DRESSMAKING SCISSORS
- MATCHING THREAD
- SEAM RIPPER

1
Unpick the hems of the dish towels with the seam ripper. There is no need to press the unpicked hems as the folds will be useful for making flat seams.

2
Put the dish towels together in pairs and join the three pairs of towels using a flat seam (see page 26) [diagram 2.a]. Then join the resulting three strips together using flat seams [diagram 2.b].

3
Make a $\frac{1}{2}$-inch (1-cm) double hem around the edge of the tablecloth with non-mitered or mitered corners (see page 30), and machine $\frac{1}{12}$ inch (2 mm) from the edge [diagram 3].

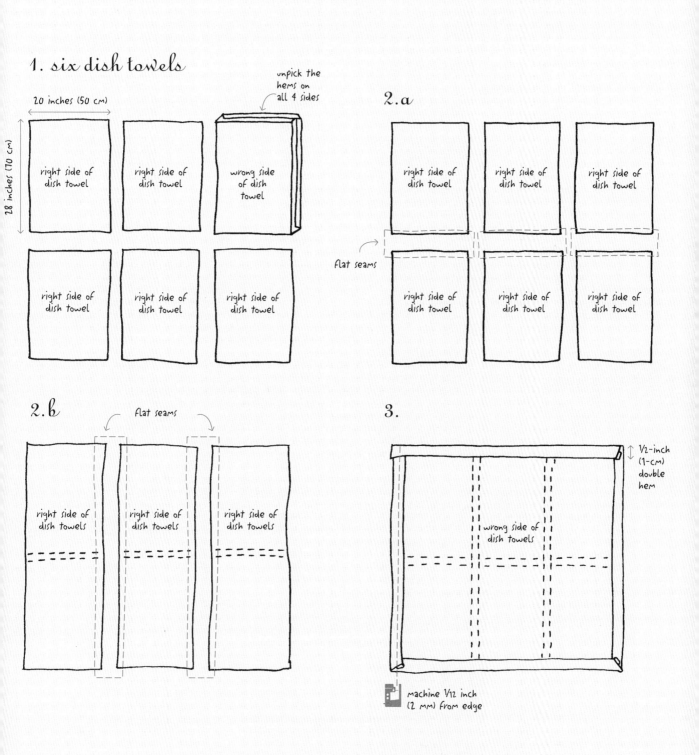

1. six dish towels

20 inches (50 cm)

28 inches (70 cm)

unpick the hems on all 4 sides

right side of dish towel

right side of dish towel

wrong side of dish towel

right side of dish towel

right side of dish towel

right side of dish towel

2.a

right side of dish towel

right side of dish towel

right side of dish towel

flat seams

right side of dish towel

right side of dish towel

right side of dish towel

2.b

flat seams

right side of dish towels

right side of dish towels

right side of dish towels

3.

½-inch (1-cm) double hem

wrong side of dish towels

machine 1/12 inch (2 mm) from edge

Saturday market caddy

Shopping list

- AN OLD CADDY AND ITS BAG
- 2/3 YARD (60 CM) OILCLOTH, 57 INCHES (145 CM) WIDE
- 4 YARDS (3.6 M) MATCHING BIAS BINDING, 1/2-INCH (1-CM) WIDE
- 10 EYELETS, 1/8 INCH (3 MM) IN DIAMETER, AND SPECIAL EYELET PLIERS
- 32 INCHES (80 CM) RED CORD
- FLAT PIECE OF WOOD, CUT TO THE SAME SIZE AS THE BASE OF THE BAG

Sewing box

- TAILOR'S CHALK OR DRESSMAKER'S WHITE MARKING PENCIL
- LONG RULER
- DRESSMAKING SCISSORS
- MATCHING THREAD

Before you start

Remove and unpick the original bag of your caddy. Dismantle the two metal clips at the back of the flap. Clean the metal frame.

NB: Don't pin oilcloth as the pinholes will stay in the cloth!

1

Using the pieces of the original bag as a template, draw the pattern of the bag on the wrong side of the oilcloth [diagram 1.a]. Cut out the various pieces. Fold down the top of the two rectangles that will form the body of the bag, to make a 1¼-inch (3-cm) turned-under hem [diagram 1.b]. Topstitch 1/16 inch (1 mm) from the top and bottom edges of this hem.

2

Put the two rectangles together, right sides facing, and machine each side ½ inch (1 cm) from the edge using a medium-length straight stitch. Trim the seam to ¼ inch (5 mm) [diagram 2.a]. Sew on the base in the same way. Cover the visible side seams with bias binding (see page 32) [diagram 2.b].

3

For the flap, place the facing on the flap, wrong sides together. On the right side of the oilcloth, sew the bias binding around the edge of the flap 1/16 inch (1 mm) from the edge. To ensure the seam stays even, it's best to baste the binding by hand with a large stitch every ½ inch (1 cm) before machine stitching slowly.

4

Attach the flap near the facing and the upper line of topstitching on the turned-under hem of the bag. Use the original bag to help you attach the two clips to the back of the caddy, then fix the eyelets and thread the cord through them. Place the flat piece of wood inside the base of the bag.

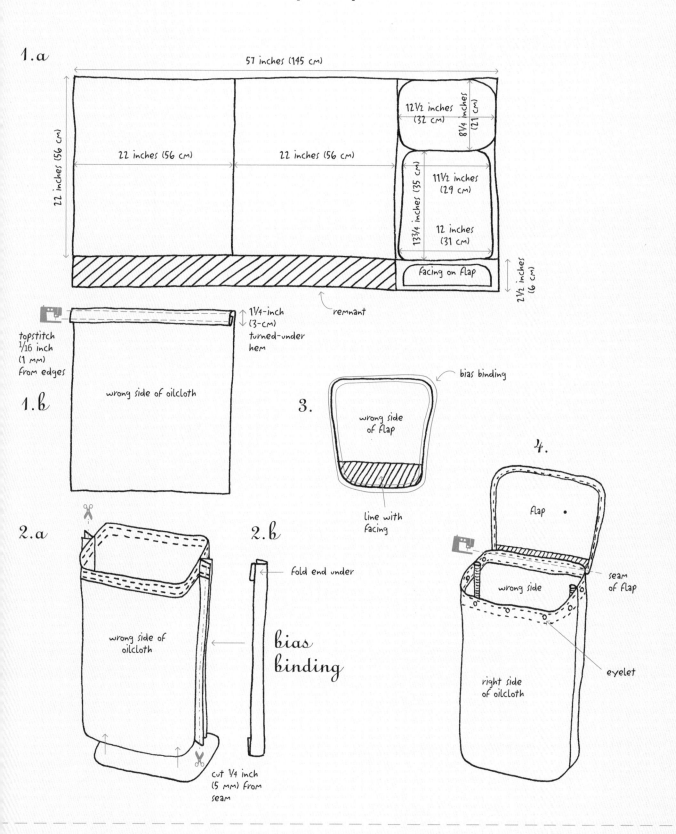

1.a

57 inches (145 cm)

22 inches (56 cm)

22 inches (56 cm)

22 inches (56 cm)

12½ inches (32 cm)

8¼ inches (21 cm)

11½ inches (29 cm)

13¾ inches (35 cm)

12 inches (31 cm)

facing on flap

2½ inches (6 cm)

remnant

1.b

topstitch 1/16 inch (1 mm) from edges

1¼-inch (3-cm) turned-under hem

wrong side of oilcloth

3.

bias binding

wrong side of flap

line with facing

4.

flap

seam of flap

wrong side

eyelet

right side of oilcloth

2.a

wrong side of oilcloth

cut ¼ inch (5 mm) from seam

2.b

fold end under

bias binding

French chef's apron

*Whether you're cooking coq au vin or la soupe à l'oignon,
you'll want this handy in the kitchen.*

Shopping list

- 2 DISH TOWELS 20 X 28 INCHES
  (50 X 70 CM)
- 2¾ YARDS (2.5 M) 1-INCH (2-CM)
  RED COTTON TAPE

Sewing box

- TAILOR'S CHALK
- RULER
- PINS
- DRESSMAKING SCISSORS
- MATCHING THREAD
- SEAM RIPPER

1

Press one of the dish towels and then draw and cut out the top of the apron (a trapezoid) to the size indicated [diagram 1.a]. From the red tape, cut the neck strap—22 inches (55 cm) long—then fold in half lengthwise and machine ¹⁄₁₆ inch (1 mm) from the edge. Make a ⅝-inch (1.5-cm) double hem along the sides of the top of the apron, inserting the neck strap ½ inch (1 cm) on each side and sewing ¹⁄₁₆ inch (1 mm) from the edge. Reinforce the backstitch on each end of the strap [diagram 1.b].

2

Unpick one of the long sides of the remaning dish towel with a seam ripper. Place the top of the apron in the center and insert in the fold of the unpicked hem [diagram 2.a]. Pin and re-stitch ¹⁄₁₆ inch (1 mm) from the edge [diagram 2.b].

3

Turn back and press, then secure the top of the apron by machining on the right side, ¹⁄₁₆ inch (1 mm) from the edge, in straight stitch.

4

Cut the remaining red tape in half to form the two apron ties. Fold ⅝ inch (1.5 cm) under at one end and sew the ties on the right side of the apron. In straight stitch, sew a rectangle ¹⁄₁₆ inch (1 mm) from the edge and then a central cross.

1.a

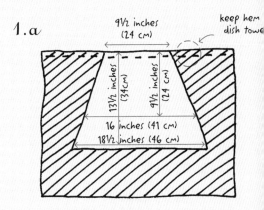

1.b   *strap*

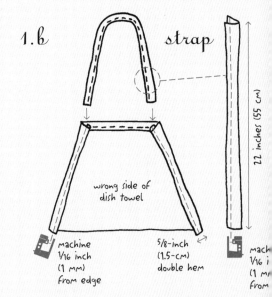

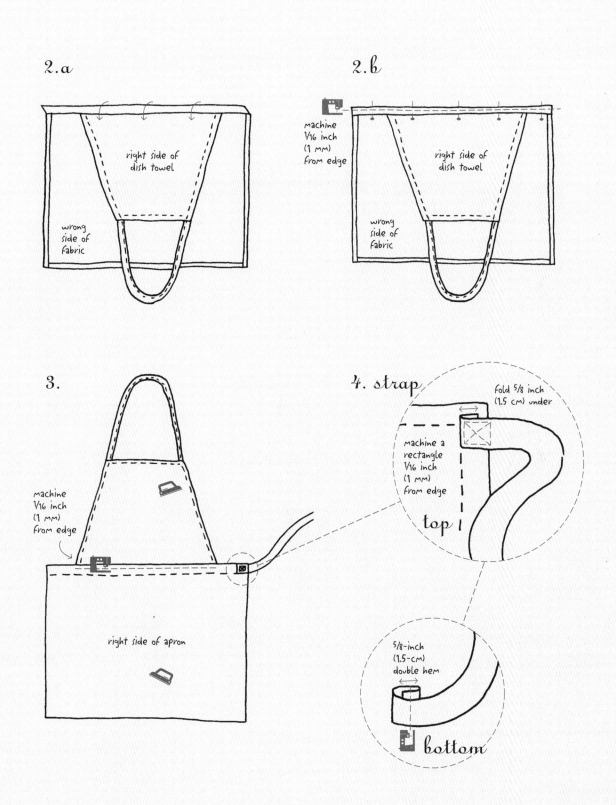

2.a

right side of
dish towel

wrong
side of
fabric

2.b

machine
1/16 inch
(1 mm)
from edge

right side of
dish towel

wrong
side of
fabric

3.

machine
1/16 inch
(1 mm)
from edge

right side of apron

4. strap

fold 5/8 inch
(1.5 cm) under

machine a
rectangle
1/16 inch
(1 mm)
from edge

top

5/8-inch
(1.5-cm)
double hem

bottom

Beautiful bath

His and Hers laundry sac (His)

Bias-trimmed blind

[INSTRUCTIONS PAGE 142] 135

Chic cosmetic case

His and Hers laundry sac (Hers)

Wraparound robe

Coquette cover-up

[INSTRUCTIONS PAGE 150] 139

Sweet chemise

[INSTRUCTIONS PAGE 154] 141

Bias - trimmed blind

Shopping list

- LIGHTWEIGHT FABRIC, SAME WIDTH AND LENGTH AS YOUR WINDOW
- COORDINATING BIAS BINDING, ENOUGH TO EDGE THE BLIND PLUS 1¾ YARDS (1.6 M) FOR THE TIES

Sewing box

- TAPE MEASURE
- PINS
- MATCHING THREAD
- NEEDLE

1

Tap a nail into each corner of the window frame and measure the width and the depth (A and B) [diagram 1.a]. Cut out the panel of fabric and two pieces of bias binding to match measurement A. Fold the binding over the raw edge of the top of the panel and baste then hand sew the binding 1⁄12 inch (2 mm) from the edge of the binding. Repeat for the bottom edge of the blind [diagram 1.b]. Cut two pieces of binding for the long sides, adding 1 inch (2 cm) to the length for the turnovers. Fold the binding over the raw edges of the blind, baste and hand sew in place [diagram 1.c], folding under ½ inch (1 cm) at each end of the binding [diagram 1.d].

2

Cut the binding for the ties into four pieces and fold under ½ inch (1 cm) at each end of the strips. Machine sew 1⁄12 inch (2 mm) from the edge of the binding [diagram 2.a]. Fold each tie in half [diagram 2.b].

3

Position the fold of the tie on the corner of the blind [diagram 3.a] and handstitch in place [diagram 3.b]. Fasten the ties to the nails.

Remember...

If your window opens in the center, you'll need to make two panels.

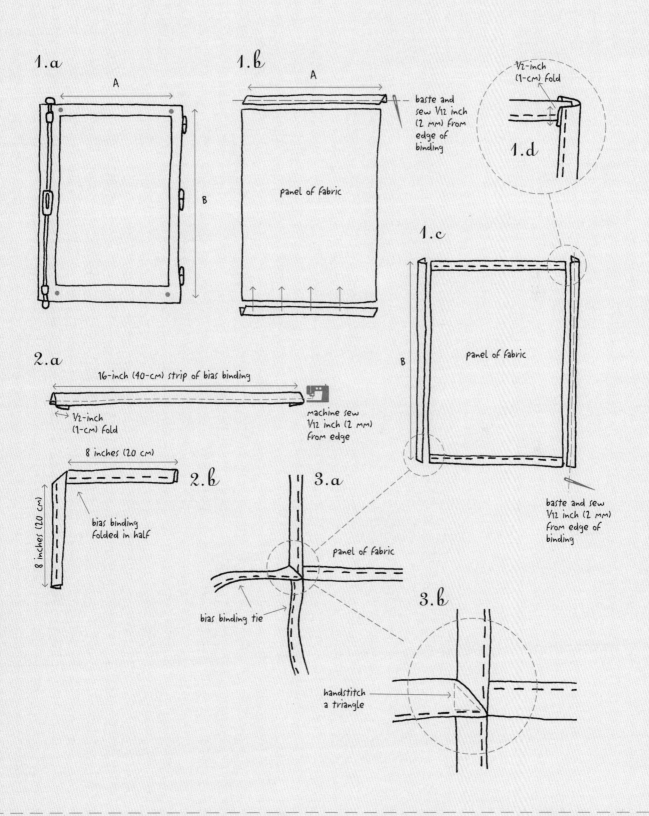

1.a

A

B

1.b

A

baste and sew 1/12 inch (2 mm) from edge of binding

panel of fabric

1.d

1/2-inch (1-cm) fold

1.c

B

panel of fabric

baste and sew 1/12 inch (2 mm) from edge of binding

2.a

16-inch (40-cm) strip of bias binding

1/2-inch (1-cm) fold

machine sew 1/12 inch (2 mm) from edge

2.b

8 inches (20 cm)

8 inches (20 cm)

bias binding folded in half

3.a

panel of fabric

bias binding tie

3.b

handstitch a triangle

Wraparound robe

1

The measurements of the pieces of printed cotton fabric will vary according to your robe. We used three rectangles 4½ x 24½ inches (12 x 62 cm) for the belt and two rectangles 6½ x 16½ inches (16 x 42 cm) for the cuffs [diagram 1.b]. Measure the belt—you'll need to make two joins [diagram 1.a]—and cuffs of your robe and adjust the measurements accordingly.

2

To make the belt, machine sew the ends of the three long rectangles together ½ inch (1 cm) from the edge, open out the seams, then turn in and press a ½-inch (1-cm) fold at each end [diagram 2.b]. Fold the belt in half lengthwise, right sides together and edge to edge (opening out the ½-inch (1-cm) folds at each end), and machine sew ½ inch (1 cm) from the edge [diagram 2.b]. Turn right side out, position the lengthwise seam in the center, and press. Then, using the safety pin, thread the original belt through the new one [diagram 2.c]. Tuck the ½-inch (1-cm) folds in at each end, machine sew ½12 inch (2 mm) from the edge, and topstitch the central seam [diagram 2.d].

3

To decorate the sleeves, press the fabric to mark the folds for the hems and cuffs [diagram 3.a]. Fold one of the sleeve rectangles in half, right sides together and edge to edge, then pin and machine sew ½ inch (1 cm) from the edge [diagram 3.b]. Turn right side out, place over one of the sleeves, turning in the folds for the inside hem, and pin [diagram 3.c]. Machine sew a circular seam ½12 inch (2 mm) from the top edge of the cuff, then handstitch the inside hem with running stitch. Trim the second sleeve to match.

1.a

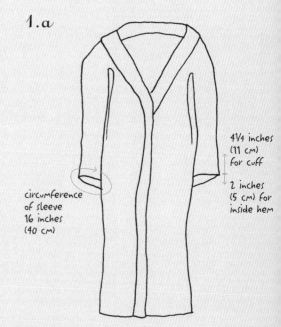

4¼ inches (11 cm) for cuff

2 inches (5 cm) for inside hem

circumference of sleeve 16 inches (40 cm)

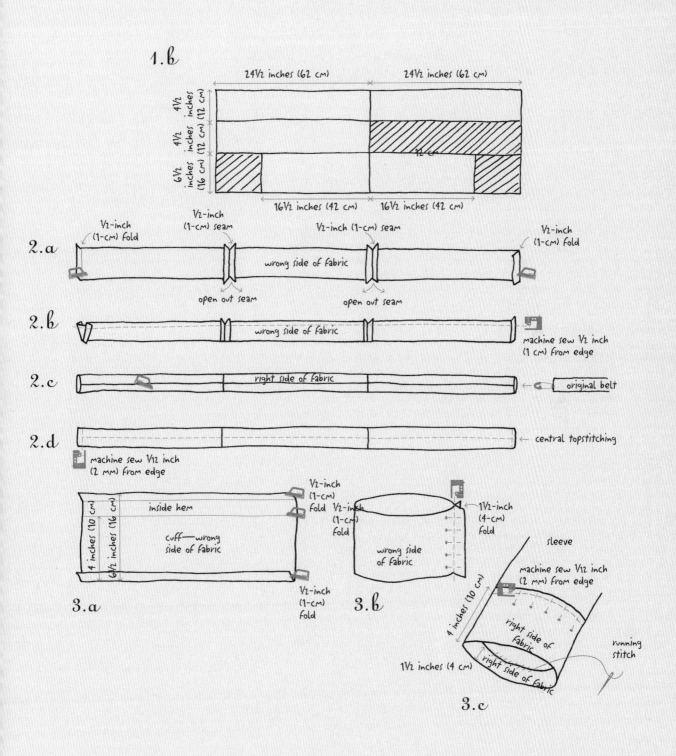

1.b

24½ inches (62 cm) 24½ inches (62 cm)

4½ inches (12 cm)

4½ inches (12 cm)

6½ inches (16 cm)

½ cm

16½ inches (42 cm) 16½ inches (42 cm)

2.a

½-inch (1-cm) fold

½-inch (1-cm) seam

½-inch (1-cm) seam

½-inch (1-cm) fold

wrong side of fabric

open out seam open out seam

2.b

wrong side of fabric

machine sew ½ inch (1 cm) from edge

2.c

right side of fabric

original belt

2.d

central topstitching

machine sew 1/12 inch (2 mm) from edge

3.a

inside hem

½-inch (1-cm) fold

½-inch (1-cm) fold

cuff—wrong side of fabric

4 inches (10 cm)

6½ inches (16 cm)

½-inch (1-cm) fold

3.b

½-inch (1-cm) fold

1½-inch (4-cm) fold

wrong side of fabric

3.c

sleeve

machine sew 1/12 inch (2 mm) from edge

right side of fabric

4 inches (10 cm)

running stitch

1½ inches (4 cm)

right side of fabric

His and Hers laundry sac (His)

Make one for whites and another for colors. All you need do is to swap around the striped and plain fabrics so you know which is yours and which belongs to your beau —what could be simpler? Thanks, guys, for helping to sort the washing in advance!

Shopping list

- ⅓ YARD (30 CM) PLAIN MEDIUM-WEIGHT COTTON, 44 INCHES (110 CM) WIDE
- 1¼ YARDS (1 M) STRIPED MEDIUM-WEIGHT COTTON, 44 INCHES (110 CM) WIDE
- 3¼ YARDS (3 M) MATCHING TAPE

Sewing box

- TAILOR'S CHALK OR DRESSMAKER'S WHITE MARKING PENCIL
- RULER
- PINS
- ROUND-HEADED PINS
- SMALL SAFETY PIN
- DRESSMAKING SCISSORS
- SEWING NEEDLE
- MATCHING THREAD
- COMPASSES
- 1 SHEET OF PAPER 12 X 17 INCHES

1

Cut out the required pieces of fabric [diagram 1.a]: two rectangles 12 x 20 inches (29 x 50 cm) from the plain cotton, two rectangles 20 x 22 inches (50 x 55 cm) and two more 3 x 20 inches (8 x 50 cm) from the striped cotton. Draw and cut out a circle 13 inches (33 cm) in diameter on the sheet of paper, then use as a pattern to cut from the remaining striped fabric. Machine sew the edges of each piece with zigzag stitch [diagram 1.b] to prevent fraying.

2

Take one of the plain pieces of fabric and pin one of the narrow striped rectangles to the top edge and the larger striped rectangle to the bottom edge, right sides together and edge to edge, and machine sew ½ inch (1 cm) from the edge [diagram 2.a]. Then do the same with the other pieces. Open out the seams of the two panels and press flat. Press a ½-inch (1-cm) fold at the top of the bag. Pin the two panels right sides together and edge to edge, and machine sew the long sides ½ inch (1 cm) from the edge, to just below the narrow band at the top [diagram 2.b].

3

Open out the side seams [diagram 3.a], and machine sew a ¼-inch (5-mm) double hem on the open edges of the top sections, ¹⁄₁₆ inch (1 mm) from the edge [diagram 3.b]. Turn down the pre-pressed ½ inch (1 cm) fold along the top edge, fold again onto the first opened seam, and baste to form the casing [diagram 3.c]. Turn right side out and machine sew ¹⁄₁₂ inch (2 mm) above the line of basting.

4

To sew the base of the bag, turn the tube wrong side out and mark the quarter circles with round-headed pins, both on the bottom of the tube and on the base circle [diagram 4.a]. Pin right sides together and edge to edge, matching up the markers, and machine sew ½ inch (1 cm) from the edge. Cut the tape in half, turn the bag right side out and thread the two tapes through the casing with the safety pin [diagram 4.b].

1.a

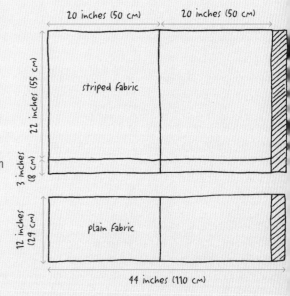

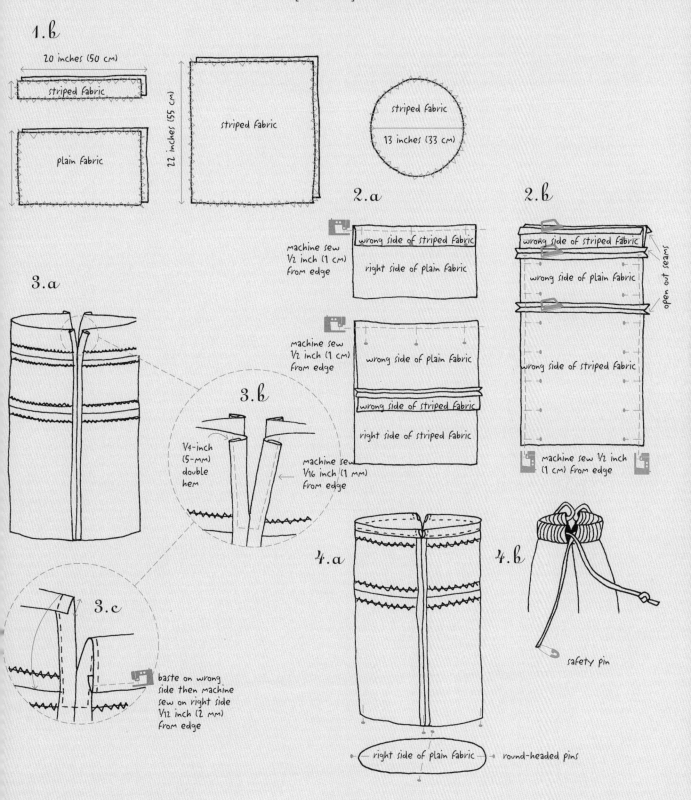

1.b

20 inches (50 cm)

striped fabric

plain fabric

22 inches (55 cm)

striped fabric

striped fabric

13 inches (33 cm)

2.a

machine sew
½ inch (1 cm)
from edge

wrong side of striped fabric

right side of plain fabric

machine sew
½ inch (1 cm)
from edge

wrong side of plain fabric

wrong side of striped fabric

right side of striped fabric

2.b

wrong side of striped fabric

wrong side of plain fabric

wrong side of striped fabric

open out seams

machine sew ½ inch
(1 cm) from edge

3.a

3.b

¼-inch
(5-mm)
double
hem

machine sew
1/16 inch (1 mm)
from edge

3.c

baste on wrong
side then machine
sew on right side
1/12 inch (2 mm)
from edge

4.a

right side of plain fabric → round-headed pins

4.b

safety pin

Chic cosmetic case

Whether you're strolling along the Seine or gallivanting across Europe, you'll always be prepared (and in style) with this sophisticated case.

Shopping list

- 2 RECTANGLES OILCLOTH 10½ X 11 INCHES (26 X 27 CM)
- 1 MATCHING ZIPPER, 10 INCHES (25 CM)

Sewing box

- TAILOR'S CHALK OR DRESSMAKER'S WHITE MARKING PENCIL
- TAPE MEASURE OR RULER
- MATCHING THREAD
- DRESSMAKING SCISSORS

1

Draw (with chalk and ruler) and cut out the two rectangles.

2

Machine sew the zipper (see page 33) along the longer sides of the oilcloth rectangles, then topstitch ⅛ inch (3 mm) from the edges on the right side of the oilcloth. Open the zipper.

3

With right sides together, machine sew the three sides of the bag in straight stitch, ¼ inch (5 mm) from the edge.

4

For the cropped corners, machine sew a seam 3¼ inches (8 cm) from the corner to form the angles at the sides of the cosmetic case. Cut off the corners ½ inch (1 cm) from the seam. Turn the case right side out through the top opening.

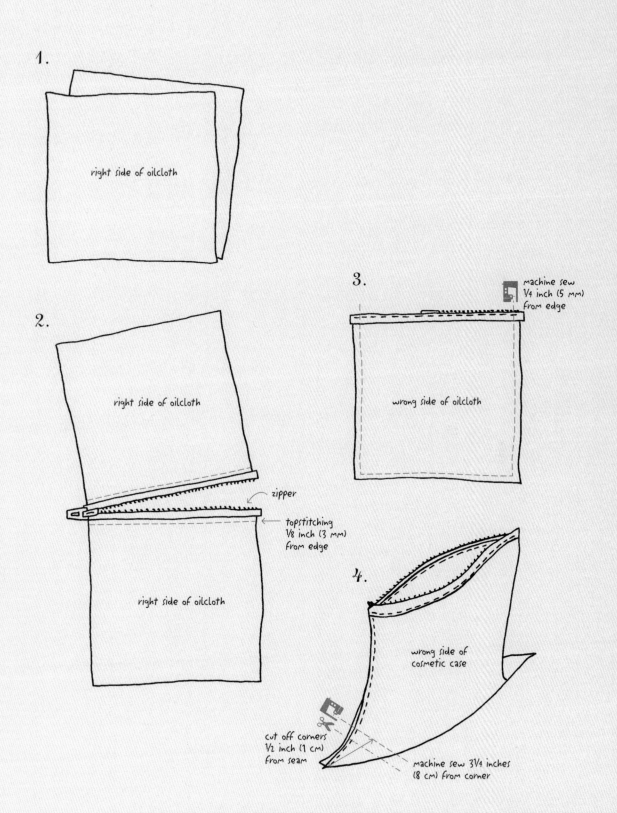

1.

right side of oilcloth

2.

right side of oilcloth

zipper

topstitching
⅛ inch (3 mm)
from edge

right side of oilcloth

3.

machine sew
¼ inch (5 mm)
from edge

wrong side of oilcloth

4.

wrong side of
cosmetic case

cut off corners
½ inch (1 cm)
from seam

machine sew 3¼ inches
(8 cm) from corner

Coquette cover-up

Whether you're lounging on a Sunday morning with an espresso and croissant or getting rea for a night on the town, you're sure to be comfortable and cute in this fashionable robe.

Shopping list

- 1¼ YARDS (1 M) WHITE TERRY CLOTH, 54 INCHES (140 CM) WIDE
- 1 SELF-COVER BUTTON, 1¼ INCHES (2.9 CM) IN DIAMETER
- 1 YARD (90 CM) X 1¼-INCH (3-CM) ELASTIC (ADJUST LENGTH ACCORDING TO CHEST SIZE)

Sewing box

- TAILOR'S CHALK OR DRESSMAKER'S WHITE MARKING PENCIL
- RULER
- PINS
- SAFETY PIN
- DRESSMAKING SCISSORS
- NEEDLE
- MATCHING THREAD

1

Take your chest measurement under the arms with the elastic, stretching it slightly and adding 1 inch (2 cm) for the seam [diagram 1.a]. Cut out a rectangle from the white terry cloth, 32 x 54 inches (80 x 140 cm), keeping the selvage [diagram 1.b].

2

Machine sew a 1-inch (2-cm) turned-under hem (see page 29) ¹⁄₁₂ inch (2 mm) from the edge, on the side opposite the selvage [diagram 2.a]. Machine sew another 3/4-inch (2-cm) turned-under hem along the bottom, ¹⁄₁₂ inch (2 mm) from the edge [diagram 2.b], and then a 1½-inch (4-cm) turned-under hem on the other long side, ¹⁄₁₂ inch (2 mm) from the edge [diagram 2.c].

3

Use the safety pin to thread the elastic through the (wider) top hem (casing) [diagram 3.a]. Secure the elastic at the ends with a backstitch [diagram 3.b].

4

Make a buttonhole through all thick-nesses (terry cloth and elastic), remembering to stretch the elastic. Cover the button (see page 34) and sew onto the front of the cover-up.

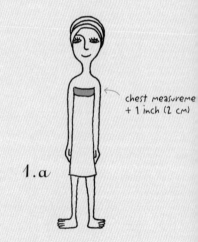

chest measureme + 1 inch (2 cm)

1.a

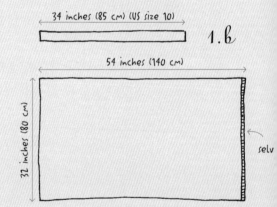

34 inches (85 cm) (US size 10)

1.b

54 inches (140 cm)

32 inches (80 cm)

selv

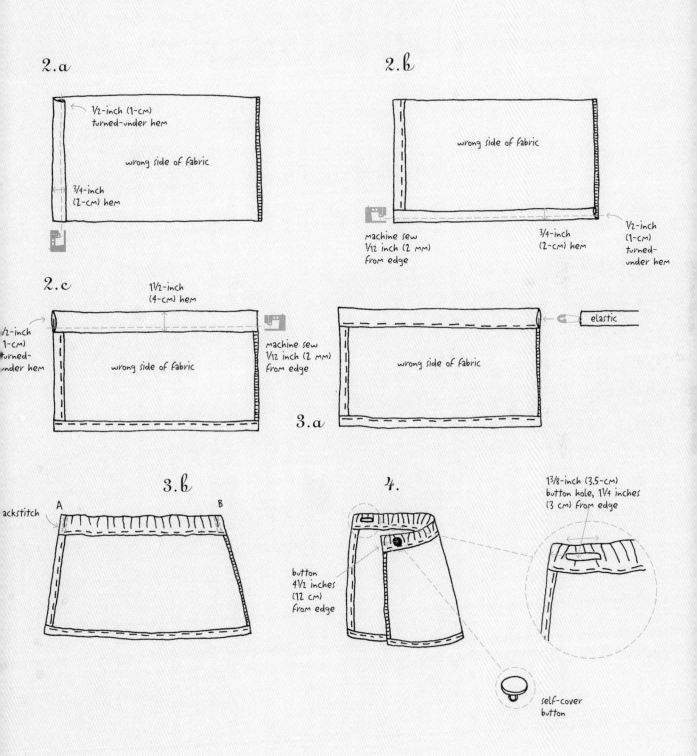

2.a

½-inch (1-cm) turned-under hem

¾-inch (2-cm) hem

wrong side of fabric

2.b

wrong side of fabric

machine sew 1/12 inch (2 mm) from edge

¾-inch (2-cm) hem

½-inch (1-cm) turned-under hem

2.c

1½-inch (4-cm) hem

½-inch (1-cm) turned-under hem

wrong side of fabric

machine sew 1/12 inch (2 mm) from edge

3.a

elastic

wrong side of fabric

3.b

backstitch

A   B

4.

button 4½ inches (12 cm) from edge

1³⁄₈-inch (3.5-cm) button hole, 1¼ inches (3 cm) from edge

self-cover button

His and Hers laundry sac (Hers)

Just like your beau's laundry bag (page 146), make one for whites and one for colors by swapping the patterned and striped fabrics around so you know which is which.

Shopping list

- ¾ yard (70 cm) striped cotton fabric, 44 inches (110 cm) wide
- ½ yard (40 cm) patterned cotton fabric, 44 inches (110 cm) wide
- 3¼ yards (3 m) matching ribbon

Sewing box

- tailor's chalk or dressmaker's white marking pencil
- ruler
- pins
- small safety pin
- dressmaking scissors
- needle
- matching thread

1

Cut out the various rectangles as shown in diagram 1.a—two rectangles 27 x 20 inches (70 x 50 cm) from the striped fabric and two rectangles 16 x 20 inches (40 x 50 cm) from the patterned fabric. Edge each piece with zigzag stitch [diagram 1.b].

2

Pin a piece of the patterned and striped fabric, right sides together and edge to edge, and machine sew ½ inch (1 cm) from the edge. Do the same for the other side [diagram 2.a]. Open out the seams of the panels and press. Then press a ½-inch (1-cm) fold along the top edge [diagram 2.b]. Pin the two panels right sides together and edge to edge, and machine sew on three sides, ½ inch (1 cm) from the edge, stopping ½ inch (1 cm) below the top edge and leaving a 1-inch (2-cm) opening on each side [diagram 2.b].

3

Open out the side seams, turn down the pre-pressed fold ½ inch (1 cm) along the top edge, and fold onto the first opened seam [diagram 3.a]. Pin and baste [diagram 3.b]. Turn the bag right side out, press the top of the opening, and machine sew 1⁄12 inch (2 mm) above the seam. Draw the lines for a 1¼-inch (3-cm) casing on either side of the 1-inch (2-cm) openings [diagram 3.c], and machine sew with two circular lines of topstitching.

4

Turn wrong side out and pin seam to seam to form the bottom corners of the bag [diagram 4.a]. Machine sew a seam 8½ inches (22 cm) from the corner, cut off the corners ½ inch (1 cm) below the seam, and finish off with zigzag stitch. Cut the ribbon in half, turn the bag right side out and thread the two ribbons through the casing with the safety pin [diagram 4.b].

1.a

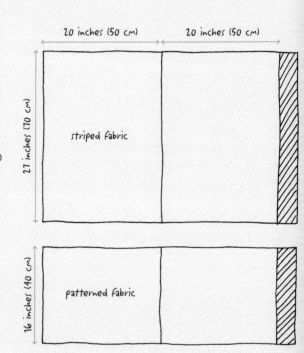

20 inches (50 cm) 20 inches (50 cm)

27 inches (70 cm)

striped fabric

16 inches (40 cm)

patterned fabric

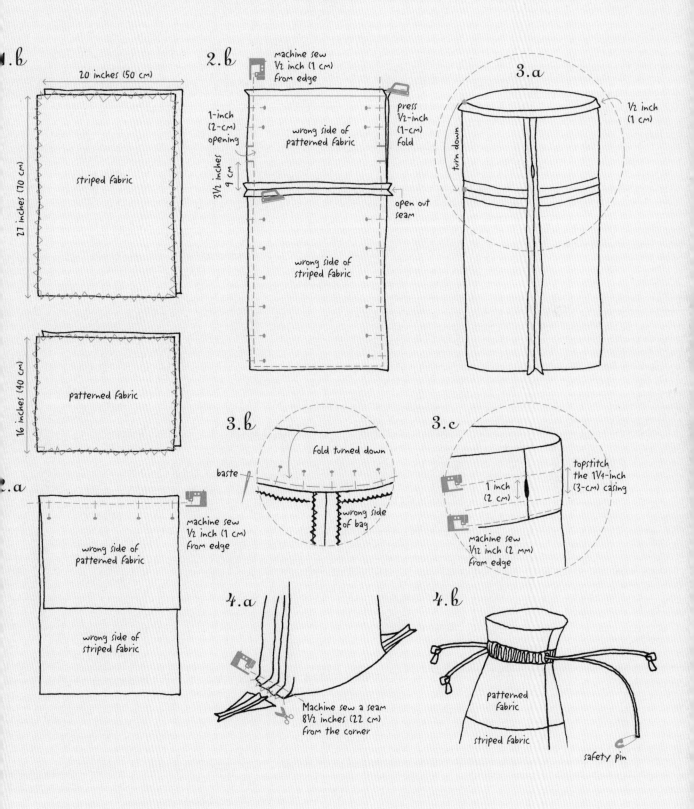

1.b

20 inches (50 cm)

27 inches (70 cm)

striped fabric

16 inches (40 cm)

patterned fabric

2.b

machine sew ½ inch (1 cm) from edge

1-inch (2-cm) opening

press ½-inch (1-cm) fold

3½ inches / 9 cm

wrong side of patterned fabric

open out seam

wrong side of striped fabric

3.a

½ inch (1 cm)

turn down

2.a

wrong side of patterned fabric

machine sew ½ inch (1 cm) from edge

wrong side of striped fabric

3.b

Fold turned down

baste

wrong side of bag

3.c

1 inch (2 cm)

topstitch the 1¼-inch (3-cm) casing

machine sew 1/12 inch (2 mm) from edge

4.a

Machine sew a seam 8½ inches (22 cm) from the corner

4.b

patterned fabric

striped fabric

safety pin

Sweet chemise

Shopping list

• 1¼ yards (1 m) fine cotton printed
  fabric, 54 inches (140 cm) wide
  (as for the wraparound robe)

Sewing box

• tape measure
• tailor's chalk or dressmaker's
  white marking pencil
• pins
• matching thread
• sewing needles

1

Using a copier, enlarge the pattern
(see page 251) to the required size,
or photocopy onto several large
sheets of paper. Cut the fabric
in half and fold each half in two,
right sides together [diagram 1.a].
Cut out the pattern and draw onto
the wrong side of the fabric.
Cut out all the pieces along the
line of the pattern [diagram 1.b],
remembering to keep the straight
grain parallel to the fold. Cut the
1½-inch (4-cm) strips from both
pieces of fabric—you will need
1 x 27-inch (70-cm) length and
2 x 11-inch (27-cm) lengths.

2

To make the ties, fold the longer strip
in half lengthwise and press [diagram
2.a]. Open out and fold in ½ inch
(1 cm) at each end [diagram 2.b].
Then fold and press the two long sides
so that they meet on the center fold
[diagram 2.c], and topstitch on all
four sides 1/12 inch (2 mm) from the
edge [diagram 2.d]. Make the two
shorter back ties in the same way.

3

Pin the front facing to the front of
the chemise, right sides together
and edge to edge, and machine sew
½ inch (1 cm) from the edge [diagram
3.a]. Do the same for the back,
inserting one end of each of the back
ties between the facing and the
fabric [diagram 3.b]. Press the seams
to flatten them, then press ½ inch
(1 cm) along the top edge of the
facings [diagram 3.c].

4

Pin the front and back of the chemise
together, wrong sides together and
edge to edge, and machine sew
¼-inch (5-mm) French seams (see
page 27) along the sides [diagram 4.a].
Leave the facings unfolded and
machine sew a ¼-inch (5-mm) double
hem (see page 29) along each of the
armholes 1/16 inch (1 mm) from the
edge [diagram 4.b].

5

Fold the pre-pressed hem along the
top edge of the back facing, turn down
onto the wrong side of the fabric,
inside the chemise, and machine a
turned-under hem 1/16 inch (1 mm)
from the edge [diagram 5.a]. Do the
same for the front, then thread the
long tie through the casing with the
safety pin [diagram 5.b]. Knot the ends
of the ties to form shoulder straps.

6

Machine sew a ¼-inch (5-mm) double
hem at the bottom of the chemise,
1/16 inch (1 mm) from the edge.

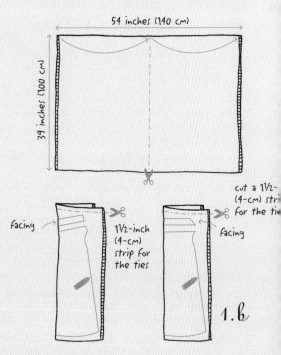

1.a

54 inches (140 cm)

39 inches (100 cm)

cut a 1½-inch
(4-cm) strip
for the tie

facing

1½-inch
(4-cm)
strip for
the ties

facing

1.b

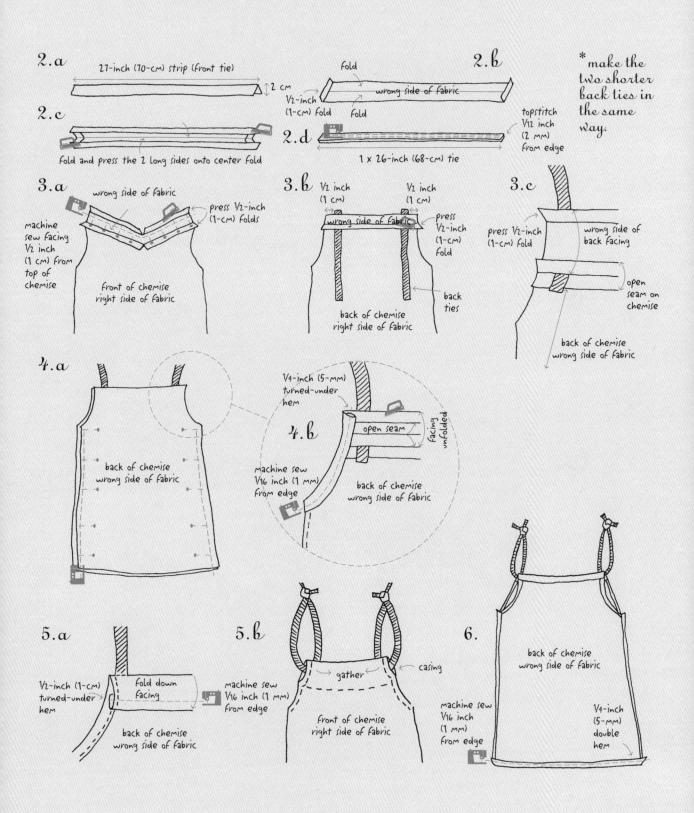

2.a 27-inch (70-cm) strip (front tie)

2 cm

2.b Fold

wrong side of fabric

½-inch (1-cm) fold

Fold

topstitch ½2 inch (2 mm) from edge

2.c Fold and press the 2 long sides onto center fold

2.d 1 x 26-inch (68-cm) tie

*make the two shorter back ties in the same way.

3.a wrong side of fabric

press ½-inch (1-cm) folds

machine sew facing ½ inch (1 cm) from top of chemise

front of chemise right side of fabric

3.b ½ inch (1 cm)   ½ inch (1 cm)

wrong side of fabric

press ½-inch (1-cm) fold

back ties

back of chemise right side of fabric

3.c wrong side of back facing

press ½-inch (1-cm) fold

open seam on chemise

back of chemise wrong side of fabric

4.a back of chemise wrong side of fabric

4.b ¼-inch (5-mm) turned-under hem

open seam

facing unfolded

machine sew ¹⁄₁₆ inch (1 mm) from edge

back of chemise wrong side of fabric

5.a ½-inch (1-cm) turned-under hem

fold down facing

back of chemise wrong side of fabric

5.b machine sew ¹⁄₁₆ inch (1 mm) from edge

gather   casing

front of chemise right side of fabric

6. back of chemise wrong side of fabric

machine sew ¹⁄₁₆ inch (1 mm) from edge

¼-inch (5-mm) double hem

Romance

Anaïs satin comforter

Lingerie carryall

Moulin Rouge beaded curtains

Chateau double drapes

Wardrobe concierge

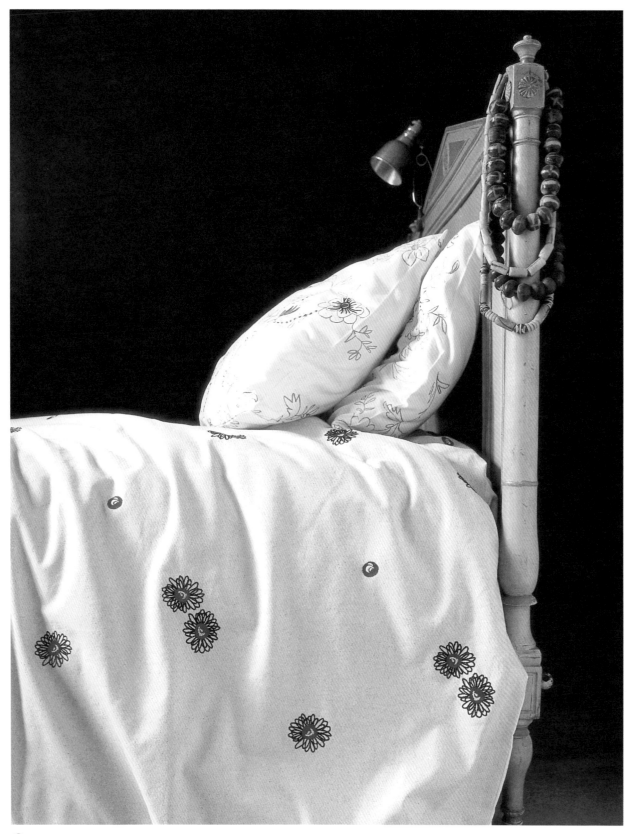

Marguerite duvet cover

[INSTRUCTIONS PAGE 166]

Embroidered pillow cases

Marguerite duvet cover

Sizes given are for a Queen-size cover (86 x 86 inches/220 x 220 cm).
Adapt the measurements to fit the size of your bed, adding 1/2 inch (1 cm) per side
for the seams and 1 inch (2 cm) for the double hem.

Shopping list

- 2³/4 yards (2.5 M) FLOWERED EMBROIDERED COTTON, 88 INCHES (230 CM) WIDE
- 2³/4 YARDS (2.5 M) COTTON FABRIC (FOR THE LINING), 88 INCHES (230 CM) WIDE

Sewing box

- TAILOR'S CHALK
- TAPE MEASURE
- PINS
- DRESSMAKING SCISSORS
- MATCHING THREAD

1

Measure, draw, and cut out the two pieces of fabric. Enlarge the pattern for the cutaway at the bottom of the comforter (see appendices, page 252), and cut out in a rounded curve.

2

Pin the two pieces of fabric right sides together and edge to edge. Machine sew ½ inch (1 cm) from the edge and finish off the double thickness of fabric with zigzag stitch. Machine sew a ½-inch (1-cm) double hem (see page 29) at the bottom of the opening. Turn right side out.

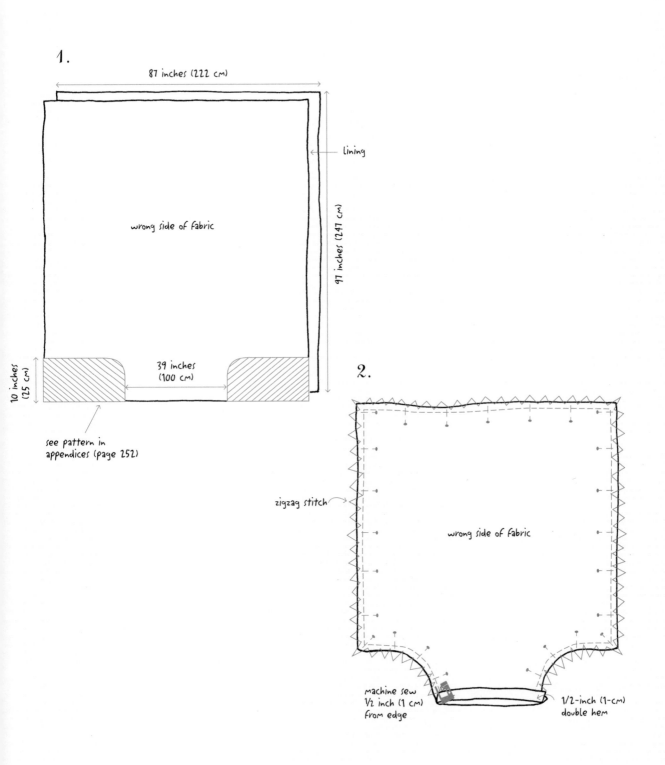

1.

87 inches (222 cm)

lining

97 inches (247 cm)

wrong side of fabric

10 inches (25 cm)

39 inches (100 cm)

see pattern in appendices (page 252)

2.

zigzag stitch

wrong side of fabric

machine sew 1/2 inch (1 cm) from edge

1/2-inch (1-cm) double hem

Embroidered pillow cases

Shopping list

- 1¼ YARDS (1 M) EMBROIDERED FLOWERED COTTON, 54 INCHES (140 CM) WIDE

Sewing box

- TAILOR'S CHALK
- TAPE MEASURE
- PINS
- DRESSMAKING SCISSORS
- MATCHING WHITE THREAD
- EMBROIDERY THREAD (BLACK, RED, BLUE)
- EMBROIDERY HOOP

1

Draw and cut out two pieces of fabric each 20 x 54 inches (50 x 140 cm), keeping the selvages.

2

Re-embroider over some of the motifs to customize the fabric, using the embroidery hoop to hold the fabric taught (see embroidery stitches, page 247). Press on the wrong side.

3

Fold the rectangle, right sides together and edge to edge, to give a double thickness of 23 inches (60 cm), [diagram 4.a]. Then fold the remaining 8 inches (20 cm) over the folded fabric [diagram 3.a]. Pin along the top and bottom edges, and machine sew ½ inch (1 cm) from the edge. Finish off the edges of the double thickness of fabric with zigzag stitch [diagram 3.b] and turn right side out. Make the other pillow case to match.

1.

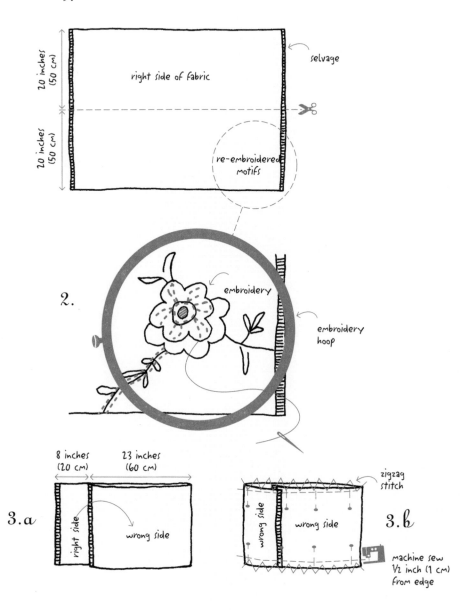

20 inches (50 cm)

20 inches (50 cm)

right side of fabric

selvage

re-embroidered motifs

2.

embroidery

embroidery hoop

3.a

8 inches (20 cm)   23 inches (60 cm)

right side

wrong side

3.b

wrong side

wrong side

zigzag stitch

machine sew ½ inch (1 cm) from edge

Moulin Rouge beaded curtains

Conjure the beauties of gay old Paris, and think of their bead necklaces every time you look out of the window. . .

Shopping list

- OPENWORK LACE PANELS, TO FIT YOUR WINDOW
- FACETED BLACK GLASS BEADS
- METAL CURTAIN RODS TO FIT THE WIDTH OF YOUR WINDOW

Sewing box

- TAPE MEASURE
- PINS
- MATCHING THREAD
- SEWING NEEDLE
- TAILOR'S CHALK

1

Fix the curtain rods onto the window and take the measurements for the drapes [diagram 1.a]. Cut out the lace panels based on these measurements [diagram 1.b].

2

Work out the number of beads for each row, leaving some without beads (1 in 3 for example) or arranging them irregularly (1 in 2, then 1 in 3) [diagram 2.a]. To sew the beads onto the panels, stitch the lace with the thread first, pass the thread through the bead, and stitch the lace again [diagram 2.b].

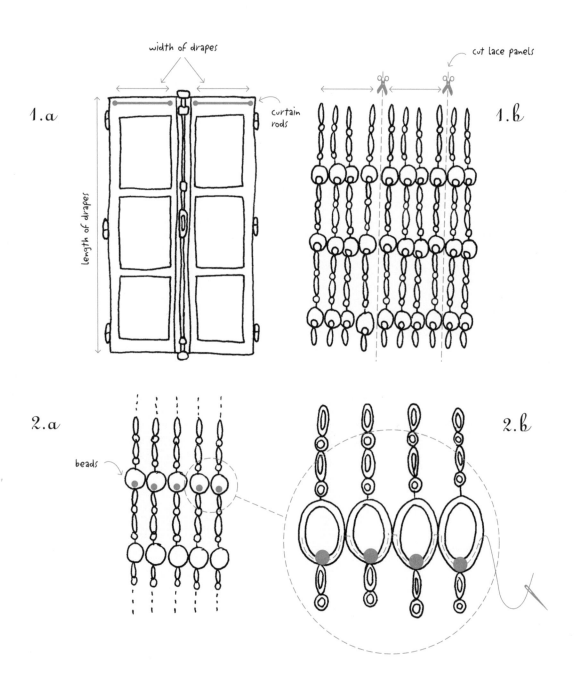

width of drapes

cut lace panels

1.a

length of drapes

curtain rods

1.b

2.a

beads

2.b

Chateau double drapes

Shopping list

- MEDIUM-WEIGHT FURNISHING FABRIC
  TO FIT YOUR WINDOW
- STRIP OF SMALL LEAD WEIGHTS SOLD BY
  THE YARD (FOR WEIGHTING THE BOTTOM
  OF THE DRAPES)
- STEEL CURTAIN ROD
- METAL CURTAIN CLIPS
- IRON-ON BONDING TAPE, 1¼ INCHES
  (3 CM) WIDE

Sewing box

- TAPE MEASURE
- PINS
- PENCIL
- MATCHING THREAD
- NEEDLE

1

Fix the steel curtain rod above the window and take the measurements for the double drapes [diagram 1.a]. Add the appropriate allowance for the type of hem—1 inch (2 cm) per side for the ½-inch (1-cm) double hems, and 3½ inches (7 cm) to the overall length for the ½ plus 1½-inch (1 plus 3-cm) turned-under hem at the top and the ½ plus 1-inch (1 plus 2-cm) turned-under hem at the bottom [diagram 1.b]. Cut out the panels for your drapes based on these measurements.

2

Draw pencil lines on the wrong side of the fabric as a guide for the different hems [diagram 2.a]. Press a strip of 1¼-inch (3-cm) bonding tape onto the top edge of each drape and machine sew the ½-inch (1-cm) double hems on the long sides. Handstitch the strip of small lead weights 1½ inches (3 cm) from the bottom of the drape, then machine sew the turned-under hems (see page 29) at the top and bottom of each drape [diagram 2.b], and attach the curtain clips to the top of the drapes.

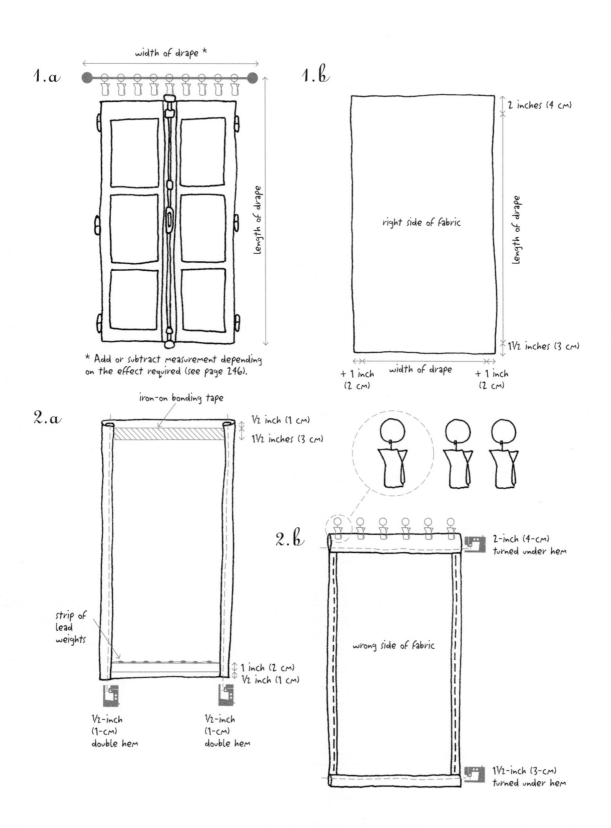

1.a

width of drape *

length of drape

* Add or subtract measurement depending on the effect required (see page 246).

1.b

right side of fabric

2 inches (4 cm)

length of drape

1½ inches (3 cm)

+ 1 inch (2 cm)   width of drape   + 1 inch (2 cm)

2.a

iron-on bonding tape

½ inch (1 cm)

1½ inches (3 cm)

strip of lead weights

1 inch (2 cm)

½ inch (1 cm)

½-inch (1-cm) double hem

½-inch (1-cm) double hem

2.b

2-inch (4-cm) turned under hem

wrong side of fabric

1½-inch (3-cm) turned under hem

Anaïs satin comforter

Don't turn your nose up at your great-grandmother's old comforter.
It may have seen better days, but why not make it a new cover!

Shopping list

FOR A TWIN COMFORTER 68 X 86 INCHES
 (175 X 220 CM):
- 5¼ YARDS (4.8 M) SATIN FABRIC,
 70 INCHES (180 CM) WIDE
- 6 SELF-COVER BUTTONS, 1¼ INCHES
 (2.9 CM) IN DIAMETER
- REMNANTS OF FABRIC FOR COVERING
 THE BUTTONS

Sewing box

- TAILOR'S CHALK
- TAPE MEASURE
- LONG METAL RULER
- PINS
- MATCHING THREAD
- SEWING NEEDLE

1

Draw (with chalk and ruler) and cut out a rectangle 187 x 69 inches (478 cm x 177 cm), keeping the selvage on one of the long sides. Machine sew the side opposite the selvage with medium-length zigzag stitch [diagram 1.a]. Press two turned-under hems, folded onto the wrong side, at each end of the fabric. Pin and machine sew with straight stitch ½2 inch (2 mm) from the edge of each hem [diagram 1.b].

2

With the chalk and tape measure, mark the position of the six buttonholes on one of the hems. Then machine sew the buttonholes (see page 34) if your machine has a buttonhole foot.

3

Fold the fabric so that the hems at either end overlap, with the buttonholes positioned under the other hem. Pin the sides and the folded ends (see diagram 3 for measurements), and machine sew the two pinned sides ½ inch (1 cm) from the edge. Turn the cover right side out through the central opening, then mark the position of the buttons with pins. You can either have the replacement buttons covered professionally or you can cover them yourself (see page 34). Sew the buttons on by hand.

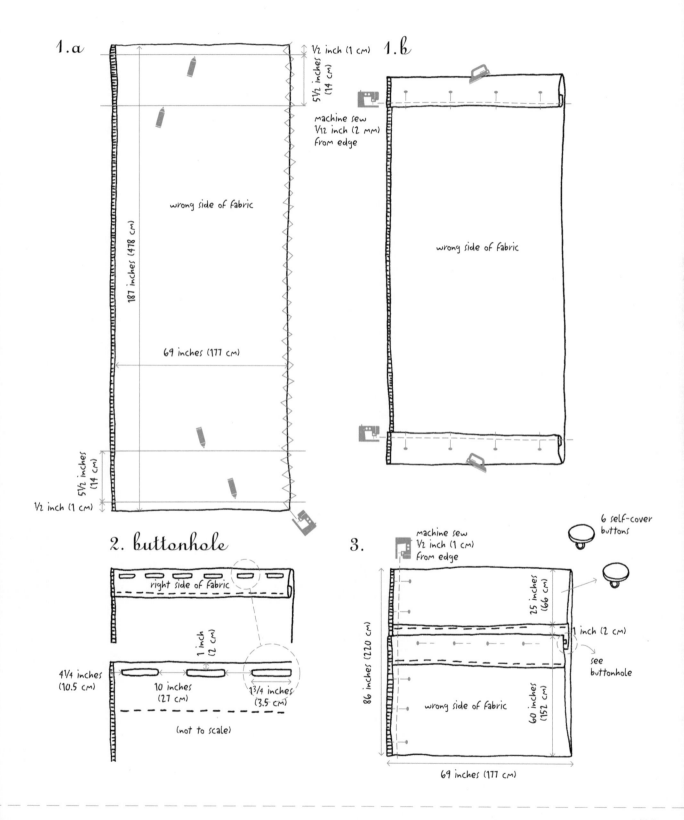

1.a

½ inch (1 cm)

5½ inches (14 cm)

machine sew 1/12 inch (2 mm) from edge

1.b

wrong side of fabric

187 inches (478 cm)

69 inches (177 cm)

wrong side of fabric

5½ inches (14 cm)

½ inch (1 cm)

2. buttonhole

right side of fabric

1 inch (2 cm)

4¼ inches (10.5 cm)

10 inches (27 cm)

1¾ inches (3.5 cm)

(not to scale)

3.

machine sew ½ inch (1 cm) from edge

6 self-cover buttons

25 inches (66 cm)

1 inch (2 cm)

see buttonhole

86 inches (220 cm)

60 inches (152 cm)

wrong side of fabric

69 inches (177 cm)

Wardrobe concierge

Shopping list

- 1⅓ YARDS (1.2 M) MEDIUM-WEIGHT FLOWERED FABRIC, 36 INCHES (90 CM) WIDE
- COAT HANGER

Sewing box

- TAPE MEASURE
- PINS
- MATCHING THREAD
- BLACK EMBROIDERY THREAD
- SEWING NEEDLE
- TAILOR'S CHALK

1

Calculate the measurements of the fabric so that the cover is the right size for the garment and cut out two rectangles. Pin the two pieces of fabric, right sides together and edge to edge, position the coat hanger at the top on the wrong side of the fabric, and draw around it [diagram 1.a]. Move the coat hanger down the fabric as far as necessary to take account of the thickness and length of the garment, adding the number of inches (cms) required for the hem —1 inch (2 cm) for a ½-inch (1-cm) double hem (see page 29) at the bottom [diagram 1.b]. Cut out ½ inch (1 cm) outside the line.

2

Re-embroider the stems of some of the flower motifs in running stitch. Then pin the two pieces of the cover, right sides together and edge to edge, and machine sew ½ inch (1 cm) from the edge. Trim the edges ¼ inch (5 mm) from the seam and edge in zigzag stitch on the double thickness of fabric [diagram 2.a]. Machine sew a ½-inch (1-cm) double hem on each side of the bottom of the cover [diagram 2.b].

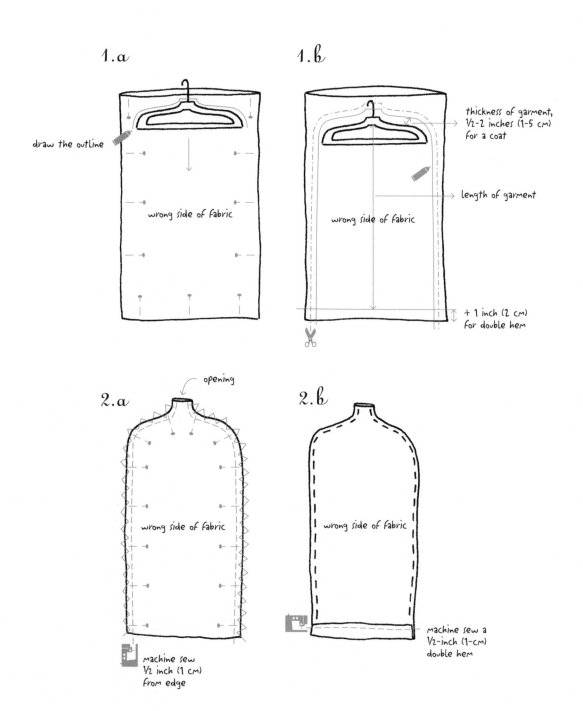

1.a

draw the outline

wrong side of fabric

1.b

thickness of garment,
½–2 inches (1–5 cm)
for a coat

length of garment

wrong side of fabric

+ 1 inch (2 cm)
for double hem

2.a

opening

wrong side of fabric

machine sew
½ inch (1 cm)
from edge

2.b

wrong side of fabric

machine sew a
½-inch (1-cm)
double hem

Lingerie carryall

Shopping list

- REMNANT OF FLOWERED LINEN FABRIC, 15 X 15 INCHES (37 X 37 CM)
- REMNANT OF PLAIN LINEN FABRIC, 15 X 45 INCHES (37 X 111 CM)
- 1¾ YARDS (1.6 M) RED RIBBON

Sewing box

- TAPE MEASURE
- PINS
- MATCHING THREAD
- NEEDLES
- SAFETY PIN

Before you start

Enlarge the pattern (see appendices, page 250) on a photocopier. Cut out four squares 15 x 15 inches (37 x 37 cm), 1 from the flowered linen and 3 from the plain.

1

Pin the pieces of fabric in pairs, right sides together and edge to edge. Cut out the pattern and draw the outline, including the markers for the openings, onto the fabric. Then cut out the various pieces ½ inch (1 cm) outside the line.

2

Pin two of the pieces—the flowered and plain fabric—right sides together and edge to edge, and machine sew ½ inch (1 cm) from the edge [diagram 2.a]. Do the same with the plain lining, leaving an opening in the bottom seam [diagram 2.b].

3

Turn the lining right side out and insert into the cover so that the right sides are together. Pin the top edges of the bag on both sides and machine sew ½ inch (1 cm) from the edge, leaving a ¾-inch (2-cm) opening on each side for the casing. Cut off the top corners and make an ⅛-inch (3-mm) slit at the top of the circular seam.

4

Turn right side out through the opening in the lining and press the bag. Draw lines to mark the seams for the casing on each side. Pin and machine sew the circular topstitching [diagram 4.a]. Cut the ribbon in half, thread through the openings of the casing with the safety pin, and knot the ends [diagram 4.b]. Close the opening in the lining by hand with running stitch.

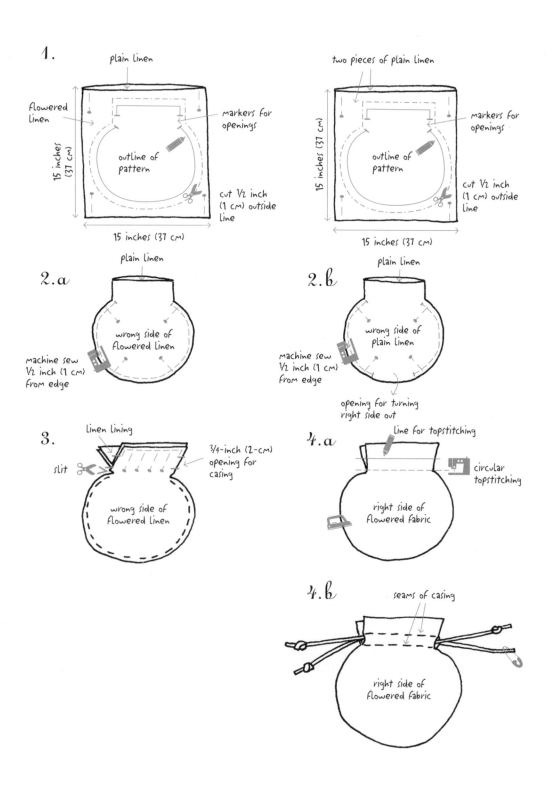

1.

plain linen

flowered linen

15 inches (37 cm)

outline of pattern

markers for openings

cut ½ inch (1 cm) outside line

15 inches (37 cm)

two pieces of plain linen

15 inches (37 cm)

outline of pattern

markers for openings

cut ½ inch (1 cm) outside line

15 inches (37 cm)

2.a

plain linen

wrong side of flowered linen

machine sew ½ inch (1 cm) from edge

2.b

plain linen

wrong side of plain linen

machine sew ½ inch (1 cm) from edge

opening for turning right side out

3.

linen lining

slit

wrong side of flowered linen

¾-inch (2-cm) opening for casing

4.a

line for topstitching

right side of flowered fabric

circular topstitching

4.b

seams of casing

right side of flowered fabric

For the little lady of the house

"Tomato" floor cushion

Pencil case à la mode

"Le Bateau" terry slippers

[INSTRUCTIONS PAGE 196]

Artists' organizer

Petite fleur duvet

Petite fleur pillow case

Ballerina drawstring bag

[INSTRUCTIONS PAGE 192]

Pencil case à la mode

Shopping list

- REMNANT OF VELVET, AT LEAST 8 x 8½ INCHES (20 x 22 CM)
- REMNANT OF FLOWERED COTTON FABRIC, AT LEAST 8 x 8½ INCHES (20 x 22 CM)
- 1 CONTRASTING ZIPPER, 8 INCHES (20 CM)

Sewing box

- TAILOR'S CHALK OR DRESSMAKER'S WHITE MARKING PENCIL
- TAPE MEASURE OR RULER
- MATCHING THREAD
- DRESSMAKING SCISSORS

1

Draw (with chalk and ruler) and cut out two rectangles measuring 4 x 8½ inches (10 x 22 cm) from each piece of fabric.

2

Machine sew the zipper (see page 35) onto the rectangles of velvet.

3

With right sides together and edge to edge, machine sew the three sides of the case in straight stitch ½ inch (1 cm) from the edge. Trim off the corners 1/12 inch (2 mm) from the edge [diagram 3.a]. Machine sew the lining on three sides, cut off the corners, and press a ½-inch (1-cm) fold on the unstitched long sides [diagram 3.b].

4

Turn the velvet case right side out, insert the lining, and handstitch it in running stitch to the seam of the zipper.

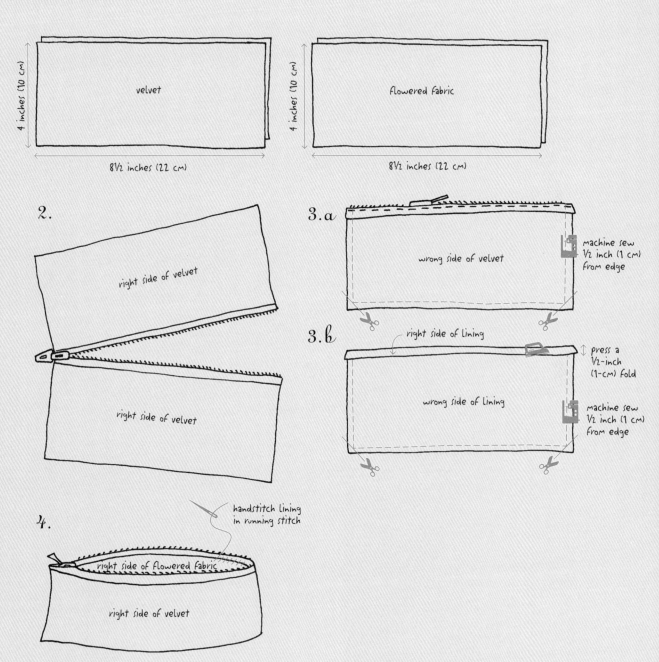

1.

4 inches (10 cm)

velvet

8½ inches (22 cm)

4 inches (10 cm)

flowered fabric

8½ inches (22 cm)

2.

right side of velvet

right side of velvet

3.a

wrong side of velvet

machine sew
½ inch (1 cm)
from edge

3.b

right side of lining

press a
½-inch
(1-cm) fold

wrong side of lining

machine sew
½ inch (1 cm)
from edge

4.

handstitch lining
in running stitch

right side of flowered fabric

right side of velvet

Ballerina drawstring bag

If your little girl dreams of becoming a ballet dancer, or simply wearing a tutu, make her a gift of this delightful bag—and the tutu to go with it, of course! You never forget your first tutu!

Shopping list

- ½ YARD (50 CM) PRINTED COTTON FABRIC, 40 INCHES (100 CM) WIDE
- REMNANT RED COTTON (LINING), 14 x 21½ INCHES (35 x 54 CM)

Sewing box

- TAILOR'S CHALK
- TAPE MEASURE
- PINS
- DRESSMAKING SCISSORS
- MATCHING THREAD

1

Draw and cut out the various pieces —one rectangle 13½ x 40 inches (35 x 100 cm) and two strips 26 x 2½ inches (65 x 6 cm) from the patterned fabric, and two rectangles 11 x 13½ inches (27 x 35 cm) from the lining fabric.

2

To make the handles, fold and press one of the long strips in half lengthwise [diagram 2.a]. Open out and fold in ½ inch (1 cm) at each end [diagram 2.b]. Then fold and press the two long sides so that they meet on the center fold [diagram 2.c], and topstitch on all four sides 1/12 inch (2 mm) from the edge [diagram 2.d]. Make the other handle to match.

3

Fold the rectangle of patterned fabric in half widthwise, right sides together and edge to edge. Then turn down 5 inches (13 cm) on each side [diagram 3], and press to mark the folds.

4

Open out the rectangle and position the handles [diagram 4.a]. Machine sew the handles so that the stitching follows the line of the original topstitching to the edge of the 5-inch (13-cm) fold [diagram 4.a]. Then turn the handles down toward the central fold [diagram 4.b]. Turn in and press ½ inch (1 cm) along one edge of each piece of lining fabric and pin the other, right sides together, to the edge of the 5-inch (13-cm) fold on the star fabric. Machine sew ½ inch (1 cm) from the edge.

5

Open out and press the seams joining the star fabric and lining. Fold and pin the two halves of the bag, right sides together and edge to edge, and machine sew ½ inch (1 cm) from the edge [diagram 5]. Turn right side out, sew the opening in the lining 1/12 inch (2 mm) from the edge, and position inside the bag.

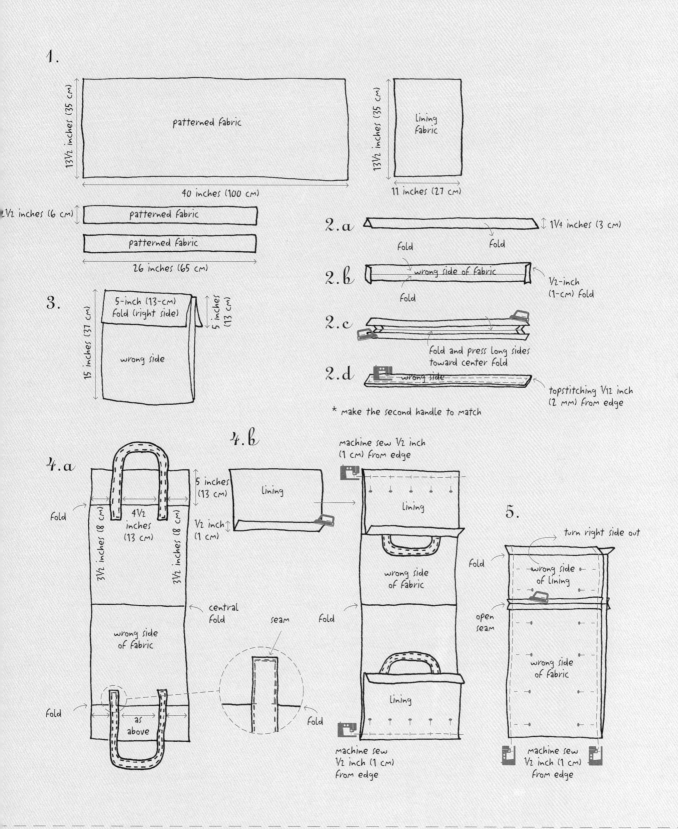

1.

13½ inches (35 cm)

patterned fabric

40 inches (100 cm)

13½ inches (35 cm)

lining fabric

11 inches (27 cm)

2½ inches (6 cm)

patterned fabric

patterned fabric

26 inches (65 cm)

2.a

1¼ inches (3 cm)

fold   fold

2.b

wrong side of fabric

½-inch (1-cm) fold

fold

2.c

fold and press long sides toward center fold

2.d

wrong side

topstitching 1/12 inch (2 mm) from edge

* make the second handle to match

3.

5-inch (13-cm) fold (right side)

5 inches (13 cm)

15 inches (37 cm)

wrong side

4.b

machine sew ½ inch (1 cm) from edge

5 inches (13 cm)

lining

½ inch (1 cm)

lining

wrong side of fabric

4.a

fold

4½ inches (13 cm)

3½ inches (8 cm)   3½ inches (8 cm)

central fold

wrong side of fabric

seam

fold

fold   as above   fold

5.

turn right side out

fold

wrong side of lining

open seam

wrong side of fabric

lining

machine sew ½ inch (1 cm) from edge

machine sew ½ inch (1 cm) from edge

"Tomato" floor cushion

The idea was to create a round cushion, but the end result was something that looked more like a tomato! Life is just full of surprises!

Shopping list

- 1³⁄4 YARDS (1.5 M) RED VELVET, 54 INCHES (140 CM) WIDE
- 1³⁄4 YARDS (1.5 M) COTTON LINING FABRIC, 54 INCHES (140 CM) WIDE
- SCRAP OF VELVET FABRIC FOR THE SELF-COVER BUTTON
- 1 SELF-COVER BUTTON, 1¹⁄4 INCHES (2.9 CM) IN DIAMETER
- 2 BAGS SHREDDED FOAM
- 3 BAGS POLYESTER FIBERFILL
- 3 YARDS (METERS) THICK CORD

Sewing box

- TAILOR'S CHALK
- TAPE MEASURE
- PINS
- DRESSMAKING SCISSORS
- MATCHING THREAD
- SEWING NEEDLE
- HEAVY-DUTY THREAD

Before you start

Using a copier, enlarge the pattern by 650 percent (see page 253). It should ultimately be 27½ inches (70 cm) high.

1

Cut out and draw the pattern on the wrong side of the fabric. Then cut out the five sections of the "tomato" ½ inch (1 cm) outside the line. Do the same for the cotton lining.

2

Use tailor's chalk to draw a horizontal line across the center of each piece of velvet, on the right side (see pattern), and then neaten the edges of each piece with zigzag stitch.

3

Pin right sides together and edge to edge, matching the horizontal lines on the five pieces of velvet. Machine sew all the pieces together ½ inch (1 cm) from the edge, leaving the seam between the last two pieces unstitched. Cut off the excess fabric at the top and bottom of the "tomato." Assemble the lining in the same way, then turn the cover and lining right side out.

4

Pin the cord inside the velvet "tomato," level with the horizontal line. Hand baste and then machine sew the ridge created by the cord using the special zipper foot [diagram 4.a]. Turn the "tomato" wrong side out and machine sew the two unstitched sections ½ inch (1 cm) from the edge, leaving a 12-inch (30-cm) opening above the ridge. Turn right side out and sew the lining together in the same way. Insert the lining through the opening and fill the cushion, placing the shredded foam in the center and the fiberfill around the edges. Close the two openings by hand using running stitch [diagram 4.b]. Cover the button (see page 34) and sew to the top of the "tomato."

1.

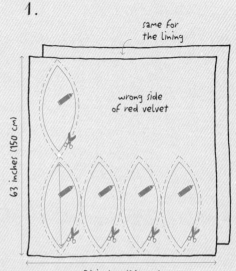

same for the lining

63 inches (150 cm)

wrong side of red velvet

54 inches (140 cm)

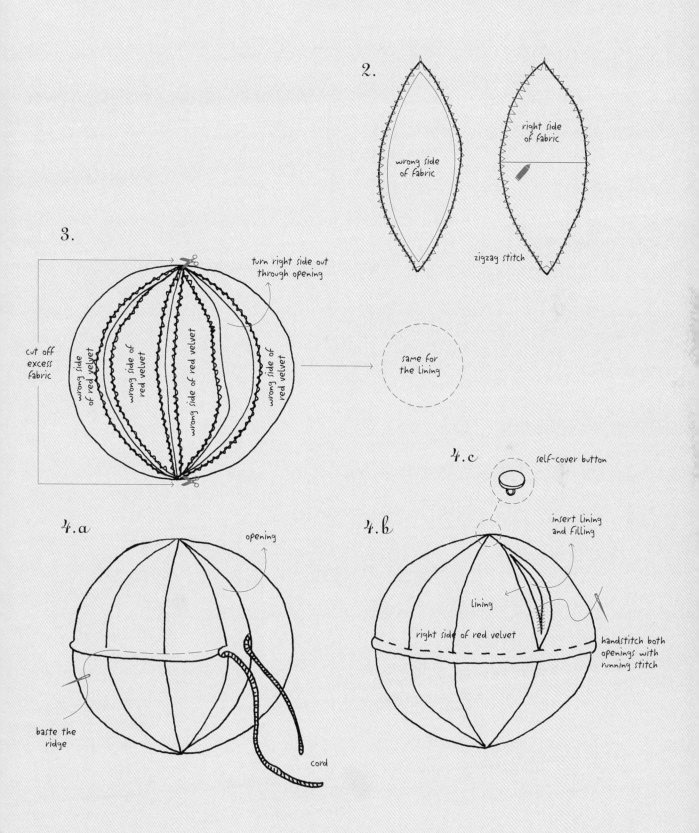

2.

wrong side
of fabric

right side
of fabric

zigzag stitch

3.

cut off
excess
fabric

turn right side out
through opening

wrong side
of red velvet

wrong side of
red velvet

wrong side of
red velvet

wrong side of
red velvet

same for
the lining

4.a

opening

baste the
ridge

cord

4.b

lining

right side of red velvet

insert lining
and filling

handstitch both
openings with
running stitch

4.c

self-cover button

"Le Bateau" terry slippers

Shopping list

- REMNANT OF RED TERRY CLOTH, 12 x 36 INCHES (30 x 90 CM)
- REMNANT OF COTTON BATTING, 12 x 36 INCHES (30 x 90 CM)
- REMNANT OF FLOWERED COTTON
- SCRAP OF IRON-ON INTERFACING (NONWOVEN)

Sewing box

- ERASABLE MARKER
- PINS
- DRESSMAKING SCISSORS
- SEWING NEEDLE
- MATCHING THREAD

1

Enlarge the pattern on page 250 on a photocopier to match the length of your little darling's shoes. Cut out and draw the patterns on the terry cloth fabric.

2

Pin the terry cloth (double thickness) right sides together, remembering to reverse the pattern for the opposite foot. Cut out the various pieces ½ inch (1 cm) outside the line [diagram 2.a]. For the 3 layers of batting, cut ⅛ inch (3 mm) inside the line [diagram 2.b].

3

Machine sew the three layers of cotton batting ¼ inch (5 mm) from the edge and then machine sew two seams running the length of the sole to hold the layers in place [diagram 3.a]. Pin the two pieces for the top part of the slipper right sides together and edge to edge. Machine sew ½ inch (1 cm) from the edge and then trim ¼ inch (5 mm) from the seam [diagram 3.b]. Turn right side out, pin, and topstitch ¼ inch (5 mm) from the edge [diagram 3.c].

4

Pin the top of the slipper to one of the soles, right sides together and edge to edge [diagram 4.a], then pin the other sole to the rest of the slipper [diagram 4.b]. Machine sew ½ inch (1 cm) from the edge, on the line, leaving an opening on the inside edge of the sole.

5

Trim ¼ inch (5 mm) from the seam near the heel [diagram 4.c]. Remove the pins, turn right side out, and insert the batting sole [diagram 4.d]. Close the opening by hand using running stitch.

Fuse 2 flower motifs to the interfacing by pressing with a hot iron [diagram 5.a]. Let cool. Cut out and handstitch to the top of the slipper [diagram 5.b].

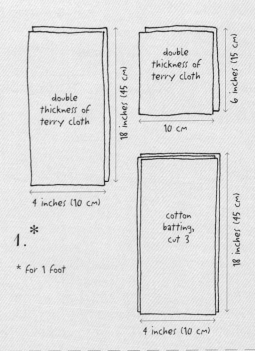

double thickness of terry cloth

18 inches (45 cm)

4 inches (10 cm)

double thickness of terry cloth

6 inches (15 cm)

10 cm

cotton batting, cut 3

18 inches (45 cm)

4 inches (10 cm)

1.*

* for 1 foot

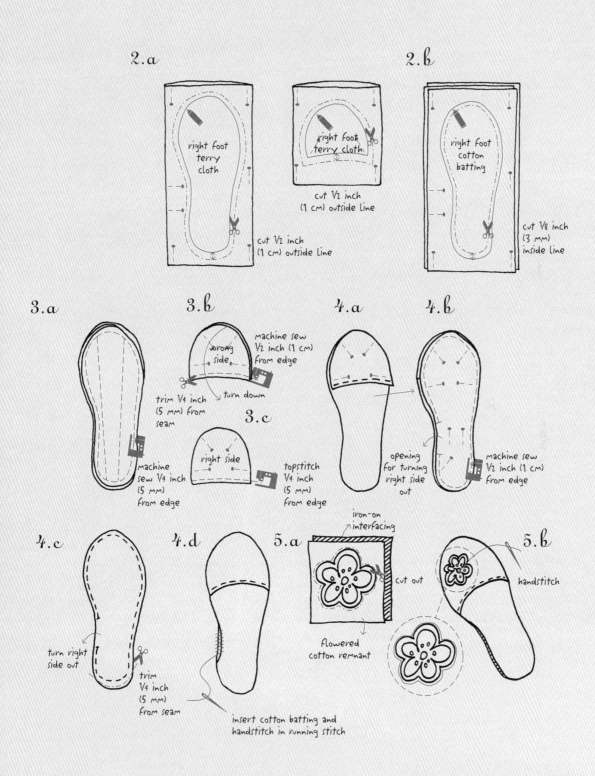

2.a

right foot
terry
cloth

right foot
terry cloth

cut ½ inch
(1 cm) outside line

cut ½ inch
(1 cm) outside line

2.b

right foot
cotton
batting

cut ⅛ inch
(3 mm)
inside line

3.a

machine
sew ¼ inch
(5 mm)
from edge

3.b

wrong
side

machine sew
½ inch (1 cm)
from edge

turn down

trim ¼ inch
(5 mm) from
seam

3.c

right side

topstitch
¼ inch
(5 mm)
from edge

4.a

opening
for turning
right side
out

4.b

machine sew
½ inch (1 cm)
from edge

4.c

turn right
side out

trim
¼ inch
(5 mm)
from seam

4.d

insert cotton batting and
handstitch in running stitch

5.a

iron-on
interfacing

cut out

Flowered
cotton remnant

5.b

handstitch

Artists' organizer

Shopping list

- ³/₄ YARD (60 CM) PLAIN, MEDIUM-WEIGHT FABRIC (FOR THE BACK), 112 INCHES (284 CM) WIDE
- 1 YARD (90 CM) FLOWERED FABRIC (FOR THE POCKETS), 48 INCHES (120 CM) WIDE
- 3 LARGE EYELETS
- 1 YARD (1 M) MATCHING BIAS BINDING

Sewing box

- TAILOR'S CHALK
- TAPE MEASURE
- PINS
- DRESSMAKING SCISSORS
- MATCHING THREAD
- EYELET PLIERS

1

Draw and cut out the various pieces —two pieces 22 x 56 inches (55 x 142 cm) for the back, and three single pieces—22 x 8 inches (55 x 20 cm), 22 x 12 inches (55 x 30 cm), and 22 x 16 inches (55 x 40 cm)—for the pockets.

2

Make a ½-inch (1-cm) double hem at the top of each of the three pockets and machine sew ¹/₁₂ inch (2 mm) from the edge. Edge the bottom of each pocket with zigzag stitch [diagram 2.a]. Position the lowest (and largest) pocket 2³/₄ inches (7 cm) from the bottom of the plain backing fabric, right sides together and upside down, and machine sew ½ inch (1 cm) from the edge [diagram 2.b]. Fold the pocket the right way up, pin onto the background, and topstitch ¹/₁₂ inch (2 mm) from the edge [diagram 2.c].

3

Do the same with the other two pockets. Then topstitch the center of each pocket and secure with a backstitch.

4

Place and pin the two pieces of plain fabric right sides together and edge to edge. Sew ½ inch (1 cm) from the edge, leaving an 8-inch (20-cm) opening at the top. Cut off the corners and turn right side out through the opening. Topstitch the edges of the organizer in green thread ¹/₁₂ inch (2 mm) from the edge.

5

To fix the organizer onto a rail, attach eyelets and ties in matching bias binding to the back. Alternatively, make a casing for a length of wood with a hole drilled at either end, thread and tie a strong piece of tape through the holes, and hang the organizer on the wall.

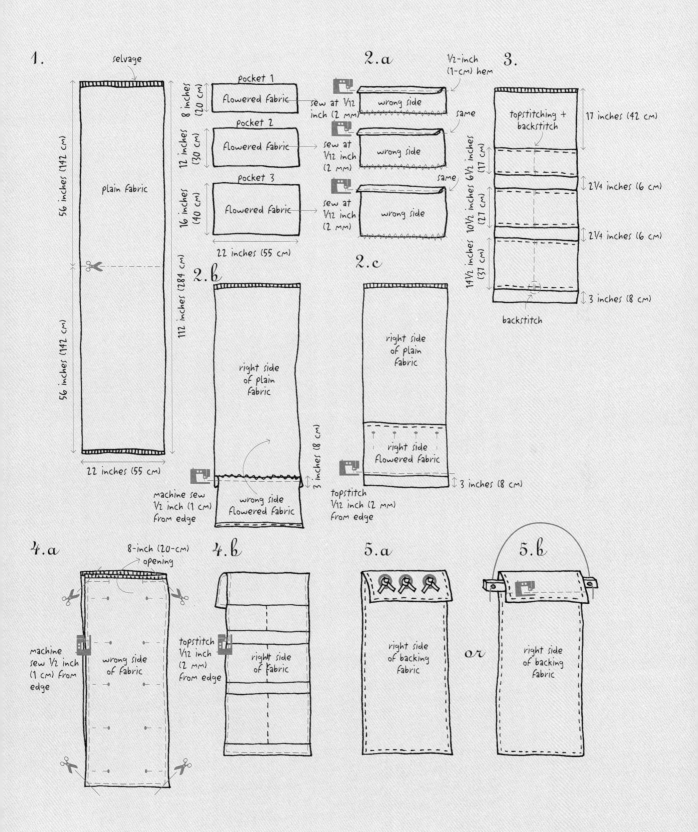

1.

selvage

plain fabric

56 inches (142 cm)

56 inches (142 cm)

112 inches (284 cm)

22 inches (55 cm)

2.a

pocket 1
Flowered Fabric
8 inches (20 cm)

sew at 1/12 inch (2 mm)

pocket 2
Flowered Fabric
12 inches (30 cm)

sew at 1/12 inch (2 mm)

pocket 3
Flowered Fabric
16 inches (40 cm)

sew at 1/12 inch (2 mm)

22 inches (55 cm)

1/2-inch (1-cm) hem

wrong side

same

wrong side

same

wrong side

3.

topstitching + backstitch

17 inches (42 cm)

6½ inches (17 cm)

2¼ inches (6 cm)

10½ inches (27 cm)

2¼ inches (6 cm)

14½ inches (37 cm)

3 inches (8 cm)

backstitch

2.b

right side of plain fabric

3 inches (8 cm)

machine sew ½ inch (1 cm) from edge

wrong side Flowered Fabric

2.c

right side of plain fabric

right side Flowered Fabric

3 inches (8 cm)

topstitch 1/12 inch (2 mm) from edge

4.a

8-inch (20-cm) opening

machine sew ½ inch (1 cm) from edge

wrong side of fabric

4.b

topstitch 1/12 inch (2 mm) from edge

right side of fabric

5.a

right side of backing fabric

5.b

or

right side of backing fabric

Petite fleur pillow case

Shopping list

- REMNANT OF FLOWERED COTTON FABRIC,
  7 X 64 INCHES (17 X 164 CM)
- REMNANT OF WHITE COTTON FABRIC
  (FOR LINING OF DUVET CASE),
  14 X 64 INCHES (37 X 164 CM)

Sewing box

- TAILOR'S CHALK
- TAPE MEASURE
- PINS
- DRESSMAKING SCISSORS
- MATCHING THREAD
- RED THREAD

1

Draw and cut out the two pieces of fabric [diagram 1].

2

Pin the flowered fabric to the white fabric, right sides together and edge to edge. Machine sew ½ inch (1 cm) from the edge, and then neaten the edge of the double thickness of fabric with zigzag stitch [diagram 2.a]. Fold this double thickness down on the wrong side, against the white fabric, and press. On the right side, sew a decorative line of large zigzag stitch in red thread on the edge of the white fabric [diagram 2.b].

3

Sew ½-inch (1-cm) double hems at each end.

4

Fold the rectangle, right sides together and edge to edge, to give a double thickness of 26 inches (65 cm), [diagram 4.a]. Fold the remaining 11 inches (29 cm) over the folded fabric. Pin the pillow case at the top and bottom [diagram 4.b], machine sew ½ inch (1 cm) from the edge, and edge the double thickness of fabric with zigzag stitch. Turn right side out.

1.

64 inches (164 cm)

7 inches (17 cm)

Flowered Fabric

14 inches (37 cm)

white fabric

64 inches (164 cm)

2.a

Finish off with zigzag stitch

hine sew nch (1 cm) n edge

wrong side of flowered fabric

right side of white fabric

2.b

decorative line of red zigzag stitch

right side of flowered fabric

right side of white fabric

3.

½-inch (1-cm) double hem

right side of flowered fabric

right side of white fabric

decorative line of red zigzag stitch

4.a

11 inches (29 cm)   26 inches (65 cm)

right side

wrong side

decorative line of red zigzag stitch

4.b

Finish off with zigzag stitch

machine sew ½ inch (1 cm) from edge

machine sew ½ inch (1 cm) from edge

Petite fleur duvet

Shopping list

- 2¼ YARDS (2 M) FLOWERED COTTON FABRIC, 56 INCHES (142 CM) WIDE
- ⅓ YARD (40 CM) RED COTTON FABRIC, 56 INCHES (142 CM) WIDE
- 2½ YARDS (2.3 M) WHITE COTTON FABRIC (UNDERSIDE OF COMFORTER), 56 INCHES (142 CM) WIDE

Sewing box

- TAILOR'S CHALK
- TAPE MEASURE
- PINS
- DRESSMAKING SCISSORS
- WHITE THREAD

1

Measure, draw, and cut out the various pieces of fabric. Enlarge the pattern for the cutaway at the bottom of the comforter (see page 252), and cut out in a rounded curve [diagram 1]. Adapt the measurements, if necessary, to fit your child's duvet.

2

Pin the red and flowered fabric right sides together and edge to edge. Machine sew ½ inch (1 cm) from the edge, and then sew a line of zigzag stitch on the double thickness of fabric [diagram 2.a]. Turn this double thickness down onto the wrong side of the red fabric and press. Then pin the double thickness on the right side, and sew a decorative line of large zigzag stitch in white thread on the red fabric [diagram 2.b].

3

Pin the red and flowered fabric to the white underside of the cover, right sides together and edge to edge. Machine sew ½ inch (1 cm) from the edge, and then edge the double thickness of fabric with zigzag stitch. Make a ½-inch (1-cm) double hem on the bottom of the opening.

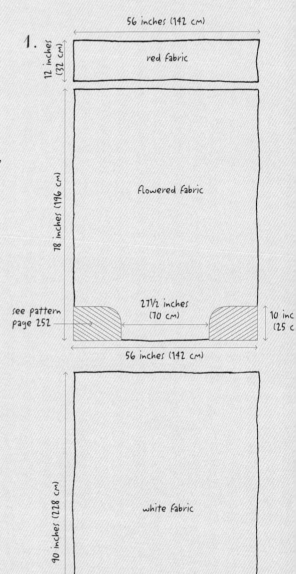

1.

56 inches (142 cm)

12 inches (32 cm)

red fabric

78 inches (196 cm)

flowered fabric

see pattern page 252

27½ inches (70 cm)

10 inc (25 c

56 inches (142 cm)

90 inches (228 cm)

white fabric

27½ inches (70 cm)

56 inches (142 cm)

2.a

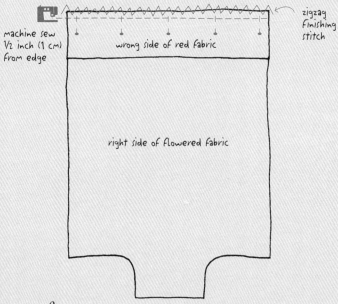

machine sew
½ inch (1 cm)
from edge

zigzag
finishing
stitch

wrong side of red fabric

right side of flowered fabric

2.b

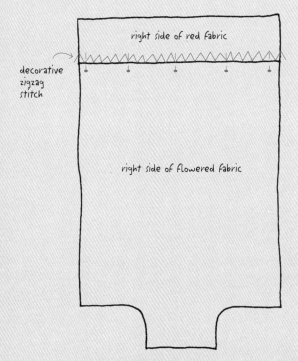

right side of red fabric

decorative
zigzag
stitch

right side of flowered fabric

3.

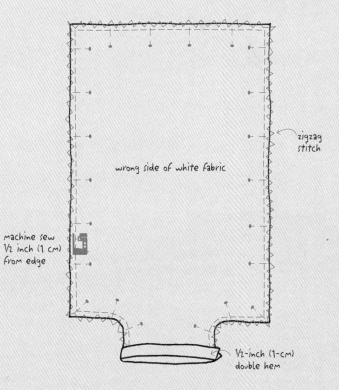

wrong side of white fabric

zigzag
stitch

machine sew
½ inch (1 cm)
from edge

½-inch (1-cm)
double hem

Out on the patio

Azure Coast sun hat

Max and the sun hat

[INSTRUCTIONS PAGE 222]

Furnishing fabric bean bag

Chic sunshade

[INSTRUCTIONS PAGE 220]

Petite garden chair

Perfect door drape

Basque hammock

Garden-artist's apron

Petite garden chair

If you've had enough of relaxing in the sunshine, why not give your favorite garden chaise a face lift?

Shopping list

- 2 RECTANGLES OF FABRIC, SAME SIZE AS THE ORIGINAL (PATTERNED FOR THE FRONT, HEAVYWEIGHT, BLACK FABRIC FOR THE BACK)

Sewing box

- TAILOR'S CHALK
- TAPE MEASURE OR RULER
- PINS
- MATCHING THREAD
- SEWING NEEDLE

Tool box

- TAPESTRY NAILS
- HAMMER
- PLIERS
- SANDPAPER
- 2 CANS SHINY BLACK SPRAY PAINT
- 1 CAN SPRAY VARNISH
- IF NECESSARY, SMALL METAL EYELETS, 1/8 INCH (3 MM) IN DIAMETER, AND SPECIAL EYELET PLIERS

Before you start

Use the pliers to remove the original tapestry nails or staples. Remove the original fabric, then clean and sand the wooden framework. Wipe clean and paint with the spray paint (two layers), then varnish (two layers).

1

Using the original fabric as a template, make a pattern allowing ½ inch (1 cm) for the seams. Draw and cut out two rectangles [diagram 1.a]. Pin right sides together and edge to edge, and machine sew ½ inch (1 cm) from the edge, leaving an 8-inch (20-cm) opening. Cut off the corners [diagram 1.b], turn right side out through the opening and press. Close the opening by hand using running stitch.

2

If the original chair has a metal tension rod marking the division between the back and the seat, fold the new fabric right sides together and edge to edge (use the original fabric as a guide) [diagram 2.a]. Pin and machine sew using straight stitch. Then fix to the framework with tapestry nails [diagram 2.b].

Handy hints

To create a stronger base for the seat, fix small metal eyelets along the fabric casing for the metal rod using special eyelet pliers (use the original holes as a guide). Choose heavyweight (furnishing) fabrics. If you buy special deck-chair fabric, you don't need a backing. Just machine sew double hems on the long sides.

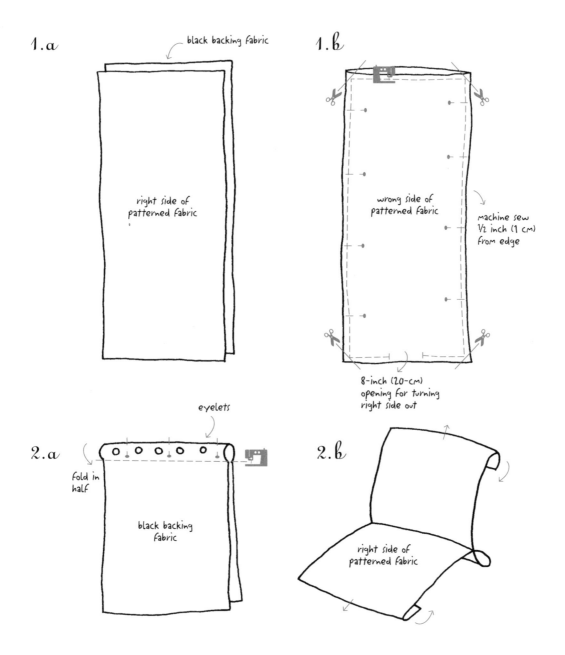

1.a

black backing fabric

right side of
patterned fabric

1.b

wrong side of
patterned fabric

machine sew
½ inch (1 cm)
from edge

8-inch (20-cm)
opening for turning
right side out

2.a

eyelets

Fold in
half

black backing
fabric

2.b

right side of
patterned fabric

Perfect door drape

Shopping list

- LIGHT- OR MEDIUM-WEIGHT FABRIC, DEPENDING ON THE SIZE OF THE DOOR
- 1 METAL CURTAIN ROD, 4 INCHES (10 CM) WIDER THEN THE DOOR
- 3 YARDS (2.8 M) MATCHING TAPE

Sewing box

- TAPE MEASURE
- PINS
- MATCHING THREAD
- NEEDLES

1

Fix the metal curtain rod above the door, and take measurements A and B for the drape [diagram 1.a]. Add 1 inch (2 cm) for the ½-inch (1-cm) double hems around the edge [diagram 1.b]. Cut out the panel based on these measurements.

2

Machine sew the ½-inch (1-cm) turned-under hems along the sides [diagram 2.a], then the ½-inch (1-cm) turned-under hems at the top and bottom [diagram 2.b].

3

Cut the tape into 7 equal pieces to make ties. Machine sew the ties ¹⁄₁₆ inch (1 mm) from the edge. Position at regular intervals along the top hem [diagram 3.a] and secure with two backstitches [diagram 3.b].

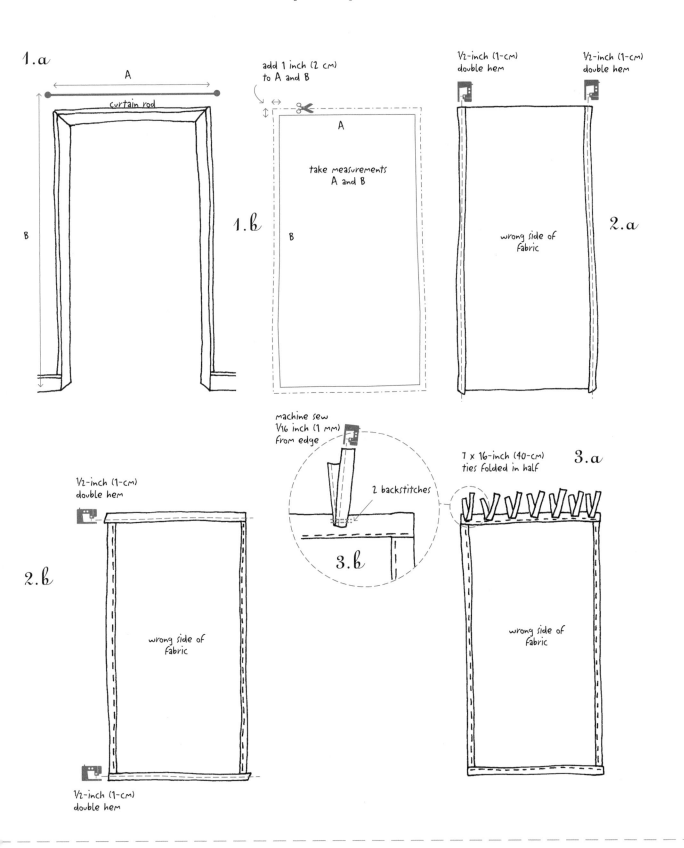

1.a

A

curtain rod

B

1.b

add 1 inch (2 cm)
to A and B

A

take measurements
A and B

B

½-inch (1-cm)
double hem

½-inch (1-cm)
double hem

2.a

wrong side of
fabric

2.b

½-inch (1-cm)
double hem

wrong side of
fabric

½-inch (1-cm)
double hem

machine sew
1/16 inch (1 mm)
from edge

2 backstitches

3.b

7 x 16-inch (40-cm)
ties folded in half

3.a

wrong side of
fabric

Furnishing fabric bean bag

Simply delightful and so simple to make!

Shopping list

- 3/4 YARD (70 CM) PATTERNED FURNISHING FABRIC, 54 INCHES (140 CM) WIDE
- 3/4 YARD (70 CM) PLAIN COTTON FABRIC, 54 INCHES (140 CM) WIDE
- 27-INCH (70-CM) LENGTH WHITE ZIPPER, SOLD BY THE YARD (METER)
- 4 X 2-LB (1-KG) BAGS POLYSTYRENE BEANS

Sewing box

- TAPE MEASURE
- PINS
- MATCHING THREAD
- SEWING NEEDLE
- ZIPPER FOOT

1

Draw (with chalk and ruler) and cut out two squares—27 x 27 inches (70 x 70 cm)—from the patterned fabric for the cover, and two squares—27 x 27 inches (70 x 70 cm)—from the cotton fabric for the cushion.

2

Neaten the edges of the two squares of patterned fabric with zigzag stitch. Pin the zipper in position (see page 35) and topstitch 1/8 inch (3 mm) from the edges.

3

Pin the two squares of plain cotton fabric, right sides together and edge to edge, and machine sew on three sides 1/2 inch (1 cm) from the edge [diagram 3.a]. Fold the opening so that the side seams are together [diagram 3.b], then machine sew 1/2 inch (1 cm) from the edge leaving a 12-inch (30-cm) opening in the center [diagram 3.c]. Turn right side out through the opening.

4

Close the zipper on the cover, leaving a 4-inch (10-cm) opening at the end. Then machine sew the cover on two sides, right sides together and edge to edge, 1/2 inch (1 cm) from the edge. Fold so that the side seams are together, and then machine sew the remaining side without leaving an opening. Open the zipper and turn right side out

5

Insert the cushion into the cover, lining up the two openings, and fill with polystyrene beads. Close the opening of the cushion by hand using running stitch, then close the zipper.

1.

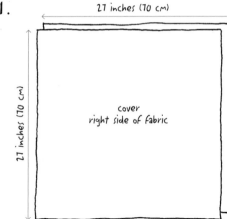

27 inches (70 cm)

27 inches (70 cm)

cover
right side of fabric

27 inches (70 cm)

27 inches (70 cm)

cushion
right side of fabric

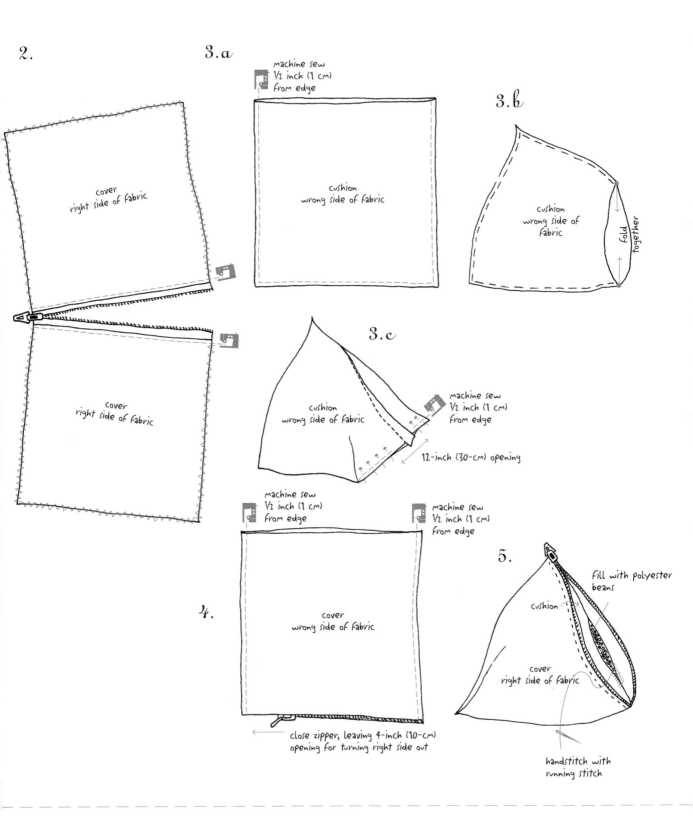

2.

cover
right side of fabric

cover
right side of fabric

3.a

machine sew
½ inch (1 cm)
from edge

cushion
wrong side of fabric

3.b

cushion
wrong side of
fabric

fold
together

3.c

cushion
wrong side of fabric

machine sew
½ inch (1 cm)
from edge

12-inch (30-cm) opening

4.

machine sew
½ inch (1 cm)
from edge

machine sew
½ inch (1 cm)
from edge

cover
wrong side of fabric

close zipper, leaving 4-inch (10-cm)
opening for turning right side out

5.

Fill with polyester
beans

cushion

cover
right side of fabric

handstitch with
running stitch

Chic sunshade

Sweet dreams, Max! I'm sure he thinks he's under some kind of giant plant!

Shopping list

- FABRIC THE SAME SIZE AND TYPE AS YOUR OLD SUNSHADE
- DECORATIVE FRINGE OR BRAID, SIMILAR TO THE EDGING ON YOUR OLD SUNSHADE

Sewing box

- TAILOR'S CHALK OR DRESSMAKER'S WHITE MARKING PENCIL
- PINS
- DRESSMAKING SCISSORS
- SEWING NEEDLE
- MATCHING THICK THREAD

Before you start

Make sure you remember how the fabric is attached to the framework so you can re-assemble the sunshade. Remove the old fabric, keeping all the small parts from the top and the ribs. Unpick one of the sections to use as a pattern, and measure to work out the amount of fabric you will need. Clean the frame and the metal base, stripping and restoring if need be with anti-rust treatment and paint.

1

Wash and press the section to be used as a pattern. Pin the pattern to the new fabric, making sure the straight grain is parallel to the selvages, and draw around the edges. Invert the pattern and repeat the process until you have the required number of sections for the sunshade.

2

Machine sew French seams (see page 27) on the long sides of each section, then neaten the whole of the lower edge with zigzag stitch.

3

Pin and machine sew the fringe on the right side of the fabric, ¼ inch (5 mm) from the edge. Re-attach the fabric to the frame.

1.

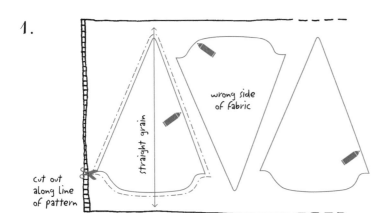

straight grain

wrong side
of fabric

cut out
along line
of pattern

2.

french seams

zigzag
stitch

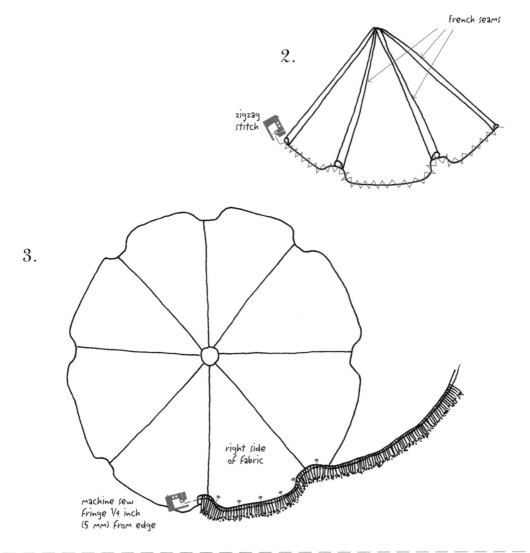

3.

right side
of fabric

machine sew
fringe 1/4 inch
(5 mm) from edge

Azure Coast sun hat

Max, put your hat on, you'll get heat stroke!

Shopping list

- 1¼ yards (1 m) PATTERNED FABRIC, 48 INCHES (120 CM) WIDE
- ⅓ yard (25 CM) LINING FABRIC, 48 INCHES (120 CM) WIDE
- 1¼ yards (1 m) GROSGRAIN RIBBON, ¾ INCH (2 CM) WIDE

Sewing box

- DRESSMAKING SCISSORS
- RULER
- TAILOR'S CHALK
- WHITE THREAD
- PINS
- COMPASSES

Note

Use round-headed pins as quarter markers on the rectangles and circles, and match them up when pinning the crown. If necessary, machine sew small pleats (tacking or basting stitch) on the rectangles so that the fabric is distributed evenly on the circle for making the crown.

Before you start

Enlarge the half-pattern (see page 253) for the hat brim as indicated. Photocopy twice and join the two pieces together with scotch tape to obtain the complete pattern. Cut out.

1

Measure the circumference of your head [diagram 1.a]. Cut out a rectangle to the measurement plus ¾ inch (2 cm) in length by 4½ inches (12 cm) wide from each of the two fabrics [diagram 1.b]. Use the compasses to draw a circle based on the circumference of your head, on each of the two fabrics, and cut out [diagram 1.c]. Fold the rectangles of patterned and lining fabric in half, edge to edge and right sides together, and machine sew ½ inch (1 cm) from the ends [diagram 1.d].

2

Fold the remaining patterned fabric right sides together and selvage to selvage. Position the pattern on the fabric taking account of the straight grain, and cut out. This gives you the 2 sections for the brim. Pin the ends of each section right sides together and edge to edge, and machine sew ½ inch (1 cm) from the edge. Open out the seams and press.

3

Pin the rectangle and circle of patterned fabric right sides together and edge to edge, and machine sew ½ inch (1 cm) from the edge. Do the same for the lining [diagram 3.a]. Pin the two sections of the hat brim, right sides together and edge to edge [diagram 3.b]. Machine sew ½ inch (1 cm) from the edge, and trim ¼ inch (5 mm) from the seam. Turn the brim right side out, press, and topstitch ¼ inch (5 mm) from the larger edge [diagram 3.c].

4

Turn the crown right side out and topstitch ¼ inch (5 mm) from the top seam. Insert the lining in the hat, wrong sides together and edge to edge [diagram 4.a]. Then pin the upturned brim and the double thickness of the crown, right sides together and edge to edge, and machine sew ½ inch (1 cm) from the edge. Position the grosgrain ribbon on this seam and machine sew 1/12 inch (2 mm) from the edge to hide the seam [diagram 4.b]. Wear the hat with the grosgrain ribbon inside.

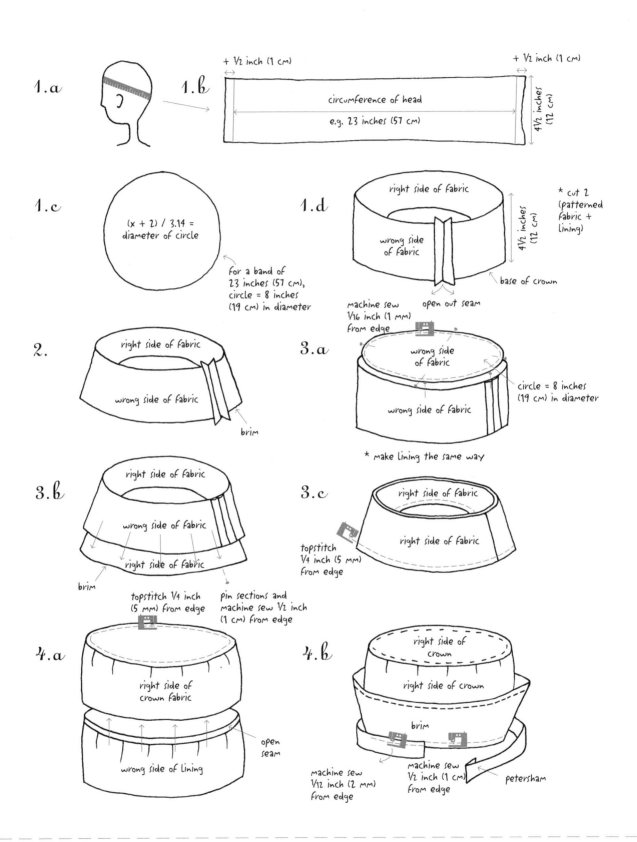

1.a

1.b + ½ inch (1 cm)   + ½ inch (1 cm)

circumference of head
e.g. 23 inches (57 cm)

4½ inches (12 cm)

1.c

(x + 2) / 3.14 = diameter of circle

for a band of 23 inches (57 cm), circle = 8 inches (19 cm) in diameter

1.d

right side of fabric

wrong side of fabric

4½ inches (12 cm)

* cut 2 (patterned fabric + lining)

base of crown

machine sew 1/16 inch (1 mm) from edge

open out seam

2.

right side of fabric

wrong side of fabric

brim

3.a

wrong side of fabric

wrong side of fabric

circle = 8 inches (19 cm) in diameter

* make lining the same way

3.b

right side of fabric

wrong side of fabric

right side of fabric

brim

3.c

right side of fabric

right side of fabric

topstitch ¼ inch (5 mm) from edge

4.a

topstitch ¼ inch (5 mm) from edge

pin sections and machine sew ½ inch (1 cm) from edge

right side of crown fabric

wrong side of lining

open seam

4.b

right side of crown

right side of crown

brim

machine sew 1/12 inch (2 mm) from edge

machine sew ½ inch (1 cm) from edge

petersham

Basque hammock

If your hammock has faded in the sun, give it a little joie de vivre!

Shopping list

- FABRIC THE SAME SIZE AND TYPE AS YOUR OLD HAMMOCK (SINGLE OR DOUBLE THICKNESS)

Sewing box

- TAILOR'S CHALK OR DRESSMAKER'S WHITE MARKING PENCIL
- PINS
- DRESSMAKING SCISSORS
- SEWING NEEDLE
- MATCHING HEAVY-DUTY THREAD

Before you start

Unpick and measure the old fabric of your hammock, making sure you can remember how to re-assemble it afterwards. If you choose a fabric that isn't designed for this type of use, you would be well advised to use a double thickness for extra strength. If you use deck-chair fabric, a single thickness will do. Simply machine sew double hems on the long sides.

1

Take account of the width of the hems, and include them in the measurements. If using a double thickness of fabric, cut out two rectangles. Pull the wooden dowels toward the loops to make it easier to attach and sew the ropes onto the new fabric.

2

Sew the two rectangles, right sides together and edge to edge, ½ inch (1 cm) from the edge, leaving a 10-inch (25-cm) opening at one end. Cut off the corners. Turn right side out through the opening and press.

3

Topstitch the long sides ¼ inch (5 mm) from the edge. Remembering how it was put together, baste the ropes individually by hand, make a double seam, and machine sew 2 rows of topstitching on the new fabric to hold the ropes in place and make the hammock more secure.

1.

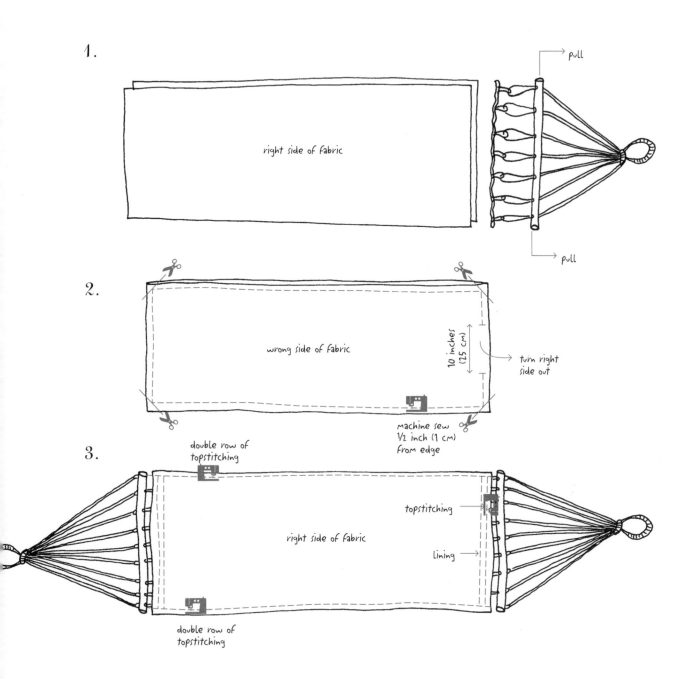

right side of fabric

pull

pull

2.

wrong side of fabric

10 inches (25 cm)

turn right side out

machine sew ½ inch (1 cm) from edge

3.

double row of topstitching

topstitching

right side of fabric

lining

double row of topstitching

Garden-artist's apron

Getting dirty never looked so pretty!

Shopping list

- ¾ YARD (70 CM) COTTON FLOWERED FABRIC, 36 INCHES (90 CM) WIDE
- PIECE MEDIUM-WEIGHT IRON-ON INTERFACING, 10 X 16 INCHES (25 X 40 CM)
- 6 YARDS (METERS) PRE-FOLDED BIAS BINDING

Sewing box

- TAILOR'S CHALK
- TAPE MEASURE OR RULER
- PINS
- MATCHING THREAD FOR BIAS BINDING
- SEWING NEEDLE
- DRESSMAKING SCISSORS

1

Using a copier, enlarge the pattern (see page 252) to the required size, or photocopy onto several large sheets of paper. Cut out the pattern, position, and pin onto the fabric. Draw (with chalk and ruler) and cut out the pieces.

2

Fuse the interfacing to the pocket [diagram 2.a] by pressing with a hot iron. Leave to cool. Then position and hand baste the bias binding (see page 32) along the top edge of the pocket, and machine sew 1/16 inch (1 mm) from the edge [diagram 2.b]. Do the same on the rounded bottom part, turning ½ inch (1 cm) under at each end, and machine sew 1/16 inch (1 mm) from the edge [diagram 2.c].

3

Baste and machine sew a 10-inch (25-cm) strip of bias binding to the top of the apron and a 46-inch (120-cm) strip around the edge of the apron, as for the pocket [diagram 3.a]. Fold the remaining strip of bias binding in half and position so that it forms the neck strap, edges the sides of top half of the apron, and forms two 20-inch (51-cm) ties. Hand baste and machine sew 1/16 inch (1 mm) from the edge. Position and pin the pocket, and follow the line of stitching for the bias binding as you machine sew the sides and bottom of the pocket to the apron. Machine sew a central line of stitching to divide the pocket in two, beginning and ending with a backstitch on the bias binding [diagram 3.b].

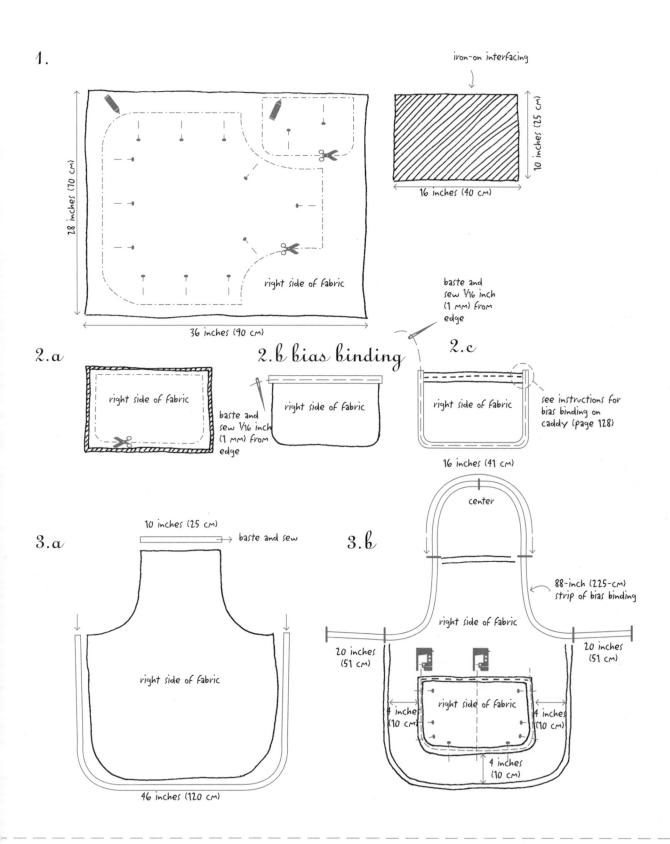

1.

iron-on interfacing

28 inches (70 cm)

36 inches (90 cm)

right side of fabric

10 inches (25 cm)

16 inches (40 cm)

baste and
sew 1/16 inch
(1 mm) from
edge

2.a

right side of fabric

baste and
sew 1/16 inch
(1 mm) from
edge

2.b bias binding

right side of fabric

2.c

right side of fabric

see instructions for
bias binding on
caddy (page 128)

16 inches (41 cm)

center

88-inch (225-cm)
strip of bias binding

3.a

10 inches (25 cm)

baste and sew

right side of fabric

46 inches (120 cm)

3.b

right side of fabric

20 inches
(51 cm)

20 inches
(51 cm)

4 inches
(10 cm)

4 inches
(10 cm)

right side of fabric

4 inches
(10 cm)

Appendices

Fabric guide: First steps

The fabrics and trims in these projects are available at fine sewing stores everywhere. For your convenience, we've listed below the manufacturer as well as the names of the actual fabrics used to create the projects in this book, but you may substitute the muslins, velvets, cotton prints, satins, silks, ribbons, and trims of your choice.

A serene, sophisticated, and elegant interior...

For this theme, a yard of the same printed fabric was used for the Tasseled shoe tote, the Boulevard butterfly trench, the Rive Gauche carryall, and the Monet flower brooch. The fabrics used for the Colette screen and the Provençal poppy lampshade were chosen for their beautiful motifs (simply irresistible!), while their warm, matching tones go perfectly with the first fabric. The French wool beret is of more humble origin—it's made from a piece of old army blanket unearthed at a Parisian flea market.

n° 1   Trimmings, Moline
n° 2   Velvet, Moline
n° 3   Muslin fabric, Zimmer + Rohde
n° 4   Woven fabric Dominique Kieffer
n° 5   Army blanket
n° 6   Printed fabric, Sahco

For addresses
see page 255.

Fabric guide: Warm and cozy

Welcoming, cozy, nostalgic...
Using the same fabric to make two
different items creates a sort of dialogue,
while the variation in format (the Cozy
Provençal quilt and the Bohemian flip flops)
shows the fabric in a completely different
light. The French deco chair and the
coordinating Vivienne velvet cushion make
use of the directionality of the stripes.
You can always make the back of the
cushions from less expensive, plain fabrics
in matching tones. The fabric used for the
Tassel tie-back is woven with very thick
threads, which makes it easy to unravel
when making the tassels.

n° 1   Printed velvet, Larsen
n° 2   Velvet, Moline
n° 3   Woven fabric, Missoni Home
n° 4   Fabric, Designer Guild
n° 5   Fabric, Designer Guild

*For addresses
see page 255.*

Fabric guide: The nesting instinct

A home décor that celebrates natural fabrics, comfort and sophistication...

For this theme, 67 inches (170 cm) of the same fabric were used for the Versailles velvet ottoman, the Velvet striped rug, and the remnants for the self-cover buttons on the Button-tufted cushion. This wonderful striped velvet and linen fabric is coordinated with such natural materials as linen (the cushion) and chair webbing (the rug). The sheen of the velvet echoes the reflections of the mother-of-pearl buttons used as a detail on the Paris opera wrap, and in profusion on the Button-backed gallery chair. You could create an entirely different but equally amazing effect by making the chair back with secondhand plastic buttons in matching tones.

n° 1   Velvet, Moline
n° 2   Silk, Designer Guild
n° 3   Velvet, Designer Guild
n° 4   Fabric, Designer Guild
n° 5   Chair webbing, Moline
n° 6   Ready-to-use grommet band, Bouchara
n° 7   Velvet, Designer Guild
n° 8   Velvet, Moline
n° 9   Linen, Moline
n° 10   Buttons, Entrée des fournisseurs
n° 11   Printed fabric, Designer Guild

For addresses
see page 255.

Fabric guide: Kitchen essentials

A graphic theme, somewhere between traditional and modern...

Combine an array of customized dish towels and a yard of designer fabric and your kitchen will have the bohemian, chic air of your favorite French café. What's more, if the idea of bedecking your kitchen with oilcloth strikes you as a little oldfashioned, I can assure you that the new, modern designer oilcloth fabrics are a real breath of fresh air!

n° 1   Printed fabric, Designer Guild
n° 2   Dish towel, BHV
n° 3   Dish towel, Monoprix
n° 4   Oilcloth, Cath Kidston
n° 5   Dish towel, Monoprix
n° 6   Dish towel, Monoprix
n° 7   Webbing, Moline

For addresses
see page 255.

Fabric guide: Beautiful bath

A fresh, natural, feminine theme...

Customize your Wraparound robe and you'll be inspired to make the delightful Sweet chemise and become a real "sleeping beauty." All the materials used for this theme are well within everyone's budget.

n° 1 Zipper, Moline
n° 2 Ribbon, Mokuba
n° 3 Fabric, Tissus Reine
n° 4 Fabric, Tissus Reine
n° 5 Fabric, Moline
n° 6 Terry cloth, Tissus Reine
n° 7 Oilcloth, Moline
n° 8 Liberty printed fabric,
      Entrée des Fournisseurs

For addresses
see page 255.

5

6

7

8

Fabric guide: For the little lady of the house

A light-hearted, tender take on classic childhood designs...

She has her own personality, lives to dance, is between 6 and 13 years old, and will love to warm her toes in red terry slippers... This theme is ready-made for your little darling, so why not surprise her? She'll be proud of you, she'll think you're amazing, and may even ask you to teach her to sew.

n° 1   Printed fabric, Sandberg
n° 2   Printed fabric, Moline
n° 3   Printed fabric, Moline
n° 4   Fabric, Tissus Reine
n° 5   Velvet, Moline
n° 6   Velvet, Moline
n° 7   Fabric, Moline
n° 8   Fabric, Moline
n° 9   Zipper, Moline
n° 10 Fabric, Moline

For addresses
see page 255.

Fabric guide: Romance

Nostalgia, charm, and a touch of glamour...
I really enjoyed combining all these wonderful fabrics that evoke some of the things I hold most dear—Japan, my grandmother, and old textiles. I fell in love with the lace for the drapes and the dark blue satin for the comforter. They're now in my bedroom, and I absolutely adore them! Sweet dreams!

n° 1   Lace, Moline
n° 2   Fabric, Designer Guild
n° 3   Satin, Tissus Reine
n° 4   Linen, Moline
n° 5   Embroidery silks, Moline
n° 6   Printed fabric, Moline
n° 7   Fabric, Moline
n° 8   Fabric, Moline

For addresses
see page 255.

Fabric guide: Out on the patio

A way to bring the garden indoors with contemporary, sunny accents...

This theme is like a huge armful of flowers, which I have not so much tried to coordinate as to highlight their diversity. I simply adore the Japanese-inspired flower motifs on the Petite garden chair, and the Furnishing fabric bean bag and Chic sunshade would be more than welcome in my garden. But what about you? Are you a hothouse plant or more of a wild flower?

n° 1   Printed fabric, Sandberg
n° 2   Printed fabric, Brunschwig & Fils
n° 3   Printed fabric, Manuel Canovas
n° 4   Printed fabric, Tissus Reine
n° 5   Fabric, Brunschwig & Fils
n° 6   Bias binding, Moline
n° 7   Trimming, Moline

For addresses see page 255.

Last thoughts

Interiors

Decide on a predominant color for the overall theme of your room and, if you're feeling adventurous, touches of a contrast color on certain objects to add pizzazz.

The same goes for materials, shapes, and style. Create the overall effect with a predominant element and then punctuate the theme with contrasting or complementary elements.

A harmonious universe needs a dialogue—a reference from one object to another—or an interplay of matching tones.

One very simple and effective way to achieve this is to use the same fabric to make different items.

Furnishing fabrics come in a wide range of qualities and prices. But who cares about price when you fall for that "must have" designer fabric? However, you can offset this cost by using it economically for items that don't take a lot of fabric, and by making the reverse side with less expensive, plain fabrics in matching tones.

When buying fabrics for making those special items, for the living room for example, think about highlighting your lovely crimson armchair by choosing coordinating fabrics in warm matching tones—crimson, scarlet, burgundy, brown, orange, ocher—to customise it and maybe even make a lap robe...

In short, everyone knows that taste and color are a matter of personal choice, so "knock yourself out!" Your interior is a reflection of your personality and anything goes!

Allowing for seams

For double drapes and sheer drapes

To take proper measurements, it's essential to fit the curtain rod first. This allows you to accurately measure the length of the fabric.

Calculating the length

This is the same for double drapes and sheer drapes. It's the length from the top of the curtain rod to the base of the drop (below the window, or to the floor) plus the allowance for the hems.

For sheer and lightweight drapes

For gathered widths, measure the length of the curtain rod, multiply it by 3, then add 2 inches (4 cm) for the ½-inch (1-cm) double hems on each side.

For flat panels, measure the length of the curtain rod, add 2 inches (5 cm)—1 inch (2.5 cm) on each side—to ensure the window is well covered and add 2 inches (4 cm) for the ½-inch (1-cm) double hems on each side.

For thick drapes

For gathered widths, measure the length of the curtain rod, multiply it by 2, then add 2½ inches (6 cm) for the ¾-inch (2-cm) turned-under hems on each side.

For flat panels, measure the length of the curtain rod, add 2 inches (5 cm)—1 inch (2.5 cm) each side—to ensure the surface of the window is well covered and add 2½ inches (6 cm) for the ¾-inch (2-cm) turned-under hems on each side.

To make a circular table cloth

First measure the table. Fold your fabric in four and hold in place with a few pins. To draw a quarter circle with the same radius as the table top, tap a nail into a flat piece of wood (stick the wood to the work surface with scotch tape), tie a piece of thread (the radius of the table top) to the nail, and fix a pencil (for drawing the quarter circle) to the end of the thread. Add ¾ inch (1.5 cm) to the radius for the ½-inch (1-cm) double hem. Pin the hem, inserting the pins at right angles to the edge, press, and machine sew near the edge.

For standard measurements, refer to mail-order catalogs.

Some basic embroidery stitches

Embroidery is much easier if you use an embroidery hoop to keep the fabric taught. Use embroidery thread and separate the strands, using 3 strands for fine embroidery and 6 strands for less delicate work.

For example, the embroidery on the clothes covers (page 162) is done in running stitch using 6 strands, while the flowers embroidered on the pillow case (page 165) are stitched with 3 strands.

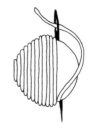

Basic satin stitch

Running stitch

Stem stitch

Encroaching satin stitch

"Hangman's knot" for curtain tie-back

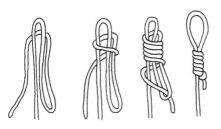

Blanket stitch

247

Glossary

Assemble

To join pieces of fabric together by stitching a seam.

Baste

An initial and temporary method of joining pieces of fabric with a basting (tacking) stitch, either by hand or by machine. For more details, see page 32.

Bias binding

A strip of fabric cut on the diagonal. Bias binding can be bought pre-folded, by the yard (or meter), from tailor's shops and department stores.

Buttonhole

A slit edged with satin stitch, either machine sewn or embroidered by hand (see "blanket stitch," page 247), through which a button is passed. For more details, see page 34.

Casing

A double row of topstitching on a fold a of fabric through which a tie is threaded.

Cool tones

Greens, blues, violets, and greys.

Coordinating fabrics

A combination of several fabrics that have motifs, colors, and textures in common.

Corners

The finished ends of the edges, which can be mitered or non-mitered. For more details, see pages 30–31.

Curved seam

A seam used when making a hat or a cylindrical cushion, for example. For more details, see page 24.

Dart

A tapered tuck made in a piece of fabric to reduce its width.

Edge to edge

The positioning of two pieces of fabric placed one against the other, right sides together, adjusting the cut edges before pinning and sewing.

Eye of a needle

The hole in a needle, at the opposite end to the point, through which the thread is passed (if necessary using a needle threader).

Flat seam

A strong type of seam used when joining fabrics that need to be resilient and hardwearing. For more details, see page 26.

Fold down . . .

. . .and press to flatten folds and seams.

French seam

A strong double seam used when making garments and items in fine, non-lined fabric. For more details, see page 27.

Hem

A finish consisting of a folded edge along the sides or bottom of fabric that is machine or hand stitched. Hems can be single, turned under, or double. For more details, see pages 28-29.

Iron-on bonding tape

A fine non-woven fabric coated with a thin film of adhesive on both sides. It is used to make non-sewn hems or to fuse two pieces of fabric together by pressing with a hot iron.

Iron-on interfacing

Non-woven fabric coated with a thin film of adhesive used to reinforce another piece of fabric by pressing with a hot iron.

"Matching tones" or "monochrome"

Shades of the same color, from the lightest to the darkest, for example.

Open out the seams

To fold down the seam allowance on each side of the seam, and press on the wrong side of the fabric. For more details, see page 22.

Oversew

To machine sew the edges of a piece of fabric in zigzag stitch to prevent them from fraying.

Pink

To make V-shaped notches in the fabric with scissors or pinking shears to prevent seams from puckering. For more details, see page 10.

Right-angle seam

A 90° seam at the corner of two pieces of fabric. For more details, see page 23.

Right sides facing or right sides together

Refers to the positioning of two pieces of fabric, with the printed side of one against the printed side of the other. The pieces of fabric should be placed edge to edge.

Running stitch

Invisible handstitching used to close an opening in a piece of work or to secure the turned-under edges of a hem. For more details, see page 35.

Selvages

The edges of the fabric that don't fray.

Straight grain

Grain running parallel to the selvages of the fabric. You need to be able to recognize it in order to position patterns correctly so that the fabric hangs properly. For more details, see page 17.

Straight stitch

Basic stitch used for joining two pieces of fabric. For more details, see page 20.

Top hem or casing

An open-ended hem through which a tie or curtain rod is threaded.

Topstitching

A line of stitching visible on the outside of a piece of work, sewn a fraction of an inch from another seam. It can be used to make a casing, or can be purely decorative. For more details, see page 25.

Warp

The fabric threads that run parallel to the selvages.

Warm tones

Reds, pinks, oranges, yellows, browns, and beiges.

Weft

The fabric threads that run perpendicular to the warp threads.

Zigzag stitch

Used to oversew the edges of a seam so that they don't fray. It can also be used as a decorative stitch. For more details, see page 20.

Patterns

LINGERIE CARRYALL

BOHEMIAN FLIP FLOPS AND "LE BATEAU" TERRY SLIPPERS

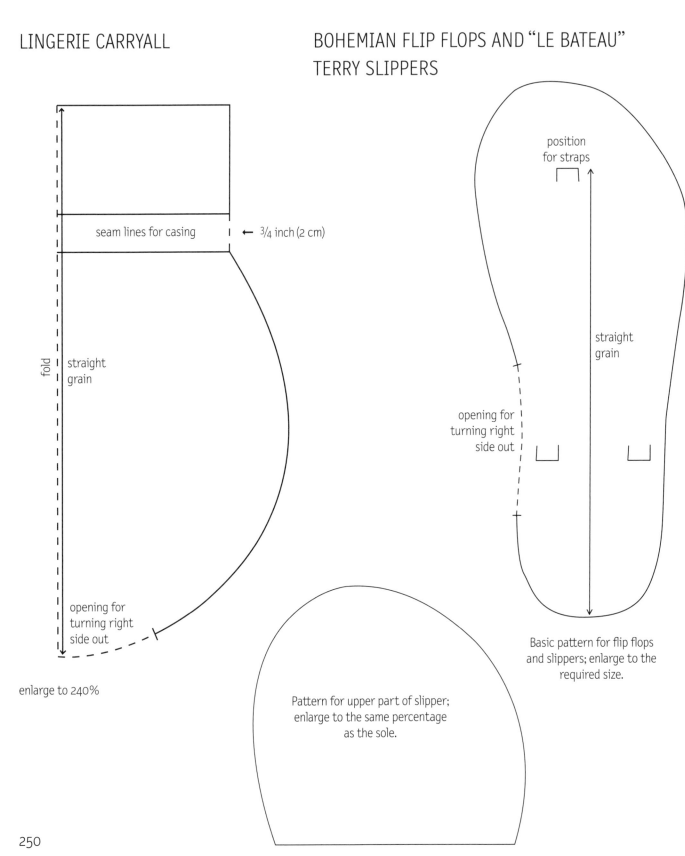

seam lines for casing ← 3/4 inch (2 cm)

fold

straight grain

opening for turning right side out

enlarge to 240%

position for straps

straight grain

opening for turning right side out

Basic pattern for flip flops and slippers; enlarge to the required size.

Pattern for upper part of slipper; enlarge to the same percentage as the sole.

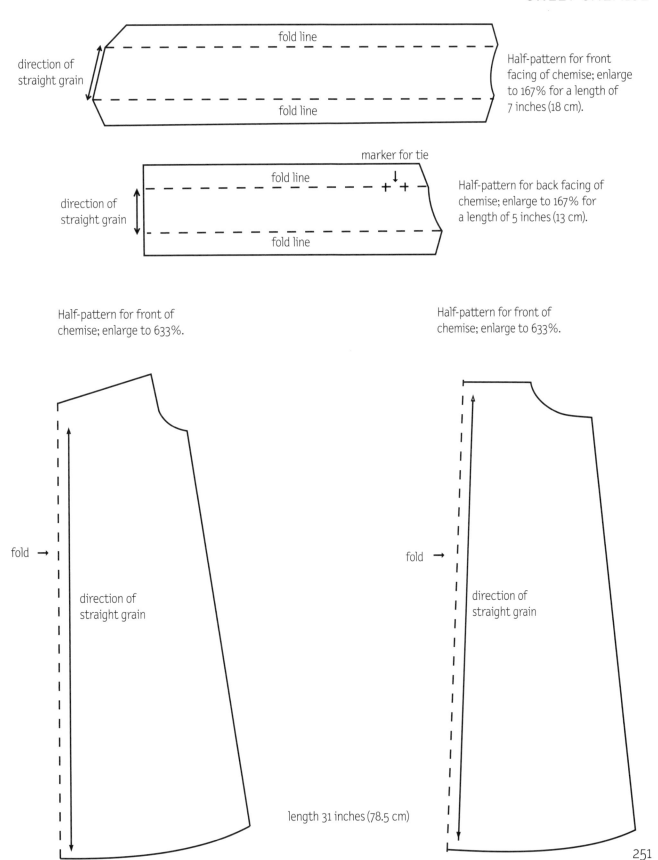

fold line

direction of straight grain

Half-pattern for front facing of chemise; enlarge to 167% for a length of 7 inches (18 cm).

fold line

marker for tie

fold line

direction of straight grain

Half-pattern for back facing of chemise; enlarge to 167% for a length of 5 inches (13 cm).

fold line

Half-pattern for front of chemise; enlarge to 633%.

Half-pattern for front of chemise; enlarge to 633%.

fold →

direction of straight grain

fold →

direction of straight grain

length 31 inches (78.5 cm)

251

GARDEN-ARTIST'S APRON

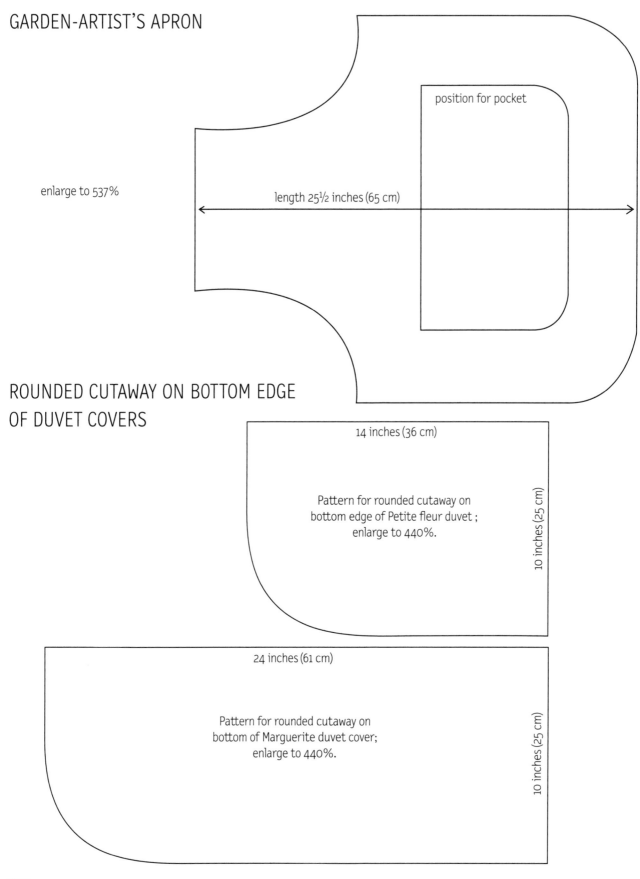

enlarge to 537%

length 25½ inches (65 cm)

position for pocket

ROUNDED CUTAWAY ON BOTTOM EDGE
OF DUVET COVERS

14 inches (36 cm)

10 inches (25 cm)

Pattern for rounded cutaway on
bottom edge of Petite fleur duvet ;
enlarge to 440%.

24 inches (61 cm)

10 inches (25 cm)

Pattern for rounded cutaway on
bottom of Marguerite duvet cover;
enlarge to 440%.

Half-pattern for brim of sun hat;
enlarge to 167%.

The pattern measurements
include ½-inch (1-cm) hems.

← fold

"TOMATO" FLOOR CUSHION

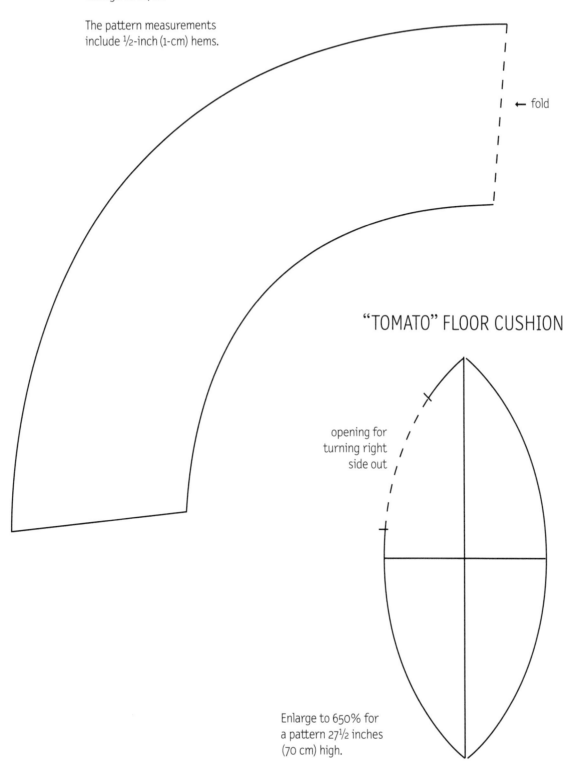

opening for
turning right
side out

Enlarge to 650% for
a pattern 27½ inches
(70 cm) high.

Index of sewing projects

A

Anaïs satin comforter 158, 174–175
Aprons:
– French chef's 110, 130–131
– Garden-artist's 213, 226–227
Artists' organizer 185, 198–199
Azure Coast sun hat 206–207, 222–223

B

Ballerina drawstring bag 188–189, 192–193
Baroque bolster cushion 86–87, 98–99
Basque hammock 212, 224–225
Bias-trimmed blind 135, 142–143
Bistro place mat 113, 120–121
Blinds:
– Bias-trimmed 135, 142–143
– Café 112, 118–119
Bohemian flip flops 89, 102–103
Boulevard butterfly trench 42, 54–55
Bourgeois bag organizer 111, 122–123
Brasserie tablecloth 114–115, 126–127
Button-backed gallery chair 63, 72–73
Button-tufted cushion 66, 80–81

C

Café blinds 112, 118–119
Chateau double drapes 161, 172–173
Chic cosmetic case 136, 148–149
Chic sunshade 209, 220–221
Colette screen 41, 52–53
Coquette cover-up 139, 150–151
Cozy Provençal quilt 88, 96–97
Cushions:
– Baroque bolster 86–87, 98–99
– Button-tufted 66, 80–81
– Vivienne velvet 93, 100–101
– "Tomato" floor cushion 182, 194–195

D

Drapes:
– Chateau double drapes 161, 172–173
– Grommetted drapes 64, 82–83
– Moulin Rouge beaded curtains 160, 170–171
– Perfect door drape 211, 216–217
Duvet covers:
– Marguerite 163, 166–167
– Petite fleur 186, 202–203

E

Embroidered pillow cases 164–165, 168–169

F

French chef's apron 110, 130–131
French cotton table runner 65, 74–75
French deco chair 91, 104–105
French wool beret pp. 43, 58–59
Furnishing fabric bean bag 208, 218–219

G

Garden-artist's apron 213, 226–227
Giverny flowered chair 116, 124–125
Grommetted drapes 64, 82–83

H

His and Hers laundry sac (Hers) 137, 152–153
His and Hers laundry sac (His) 134, 146–147

J

Jacquard lampshade 90, 106–107

L

"Le Bateau" terry slippers 184, 196–197
Lampshades:
– Provençal poppy 38, 39, 50–51
– Jacquard 90, 106–107
Lingerie carryall 159, 178–179

M

Marguerite duvet cover 163, 166–167
Monet flower brooch 45, 48–49
Moulin Rouge beaded curtains 160, 170–171

P

Paris opera wrap 68–69, 78–79
Pencil case à la mode 183, 190–191
Perfect door drape 211, 216–217
Petite fleur duvet cover 186, 202–203
Petite fleur pillow case 187, 200–201
Petite garden chair 210, 214–215
Pillow cases:
– Emboidered 164–165, 168–169
– Petite fleur 187, 200–201
Provençal poppy lampshade 38, 39, 50–5[1]

R

Rive Gauche carryall 38, 40, 56–57

S

Saturday market caddy 117, 128–129
Sweet chemise 140–141, 154–155

T

Tassel tie-back 92, 94–95
Tasseled shoe tote 44, 46–47
"Tomato" floor cushion 182, 194–195

V

Velvet striped rug 62, 70–71
Versailles velvet ottoman 67, 76–77
Vivienne velvet cushions 93, 100–101

W

Wardrobe concierge 162, 176–177
Wraparound robe 138, 144–145

Address book

Below you'll find a list of the French retailers and Parisian boutiques whose fine fabrics and accoutrements grace these pages. This book was inspired by French design (and a très chic French author); if you ever find yourself abroad, we hope you'll visit the shops below.

Fabric stores

ese stores sell many different attractive brics in all kinds of styles at prices that nge from "very reasonable" to "worth at little bit extra." Enjoy!

oline: (33) 1 46 06 14 66
Place Saint-Pierre, 75018 Paris
ww.tissus-moline.com

ssus Reine: (33) 1 46 06 02 31
Place Saint-Pierre, 75018 Paris
ww.tissus-reine.com

ouchara: (33) 2 98 43 07 33
ww.bouchara.com

ntrée des Fournisseurs: (33) 1 48 87 58 98
Rue des Francs Bourgeois, 75003 Paris
ww.entreedesfournisseurs.com

Designer showrooms

Visit these showrooms to discover beautiful treasures from the great fabric designers. Once you've made your choice you'll be directed to your nearest retailer. In some showrooms you can even place your order on the spot. You'll be in seventh heaven.

Cath Kidston: (33) 1 44 67 80 70
8 Rue St Nicolas, 75012 Paris
www.cathkidston.co.uk

Designers Guild: (33) 1 44 67 80 70
8 Rue St Nicolas, 75012 Paris
www.designersguild.com

Brunschwig & Fils: (33) 1 44 55 02 50
8 Rue du Mail, 75002 Paris
www.brunschwig.com

Dominique Kieffer: (33) 1 42 21 32 44
8 Rue Hérold, 75002 Paris

Missoni Home (in Lelièvre): (33) 1 43 16 88 00
13 Rue du Mail, 75002 Paris
www.lelievre-tissus.com

Larsen (in Manuel Canovas):
(33) 1 40 51 95 30
7 Rue Fürstenberg, 75006 Paris

Manuel Canovas: (33) 1 40 51 95 30
7 Rue Fürstenberg, 75006 Paris

Sandberg (in " Au fil des couleurs"):
(33) 1 45 44 74 00
31 Rue de l'Abbé Grégoire, 75006 Paris

Sahco-Hesslein: (33) 1 40 26 29 79
17 Rue du Mail, 75002 Paris
www.sahco-hesslein.com

Zimmer & Rohde: (33) 1 55 04 77 80
202 Rue Saint-Honoré, 75001 Paris
www.zimmer-rohde.com

Notions stores

Moline: (33) 1 46 06 14 66
1 Place Saint-Pierre, 75018 Paris
www.tissus-moline.com

La Droguerie: (33) 1 45 08 93 27
9/11 Rue du Jour, 75001 Paris
www.ladroguerie.com

L'entrée des Fournisseurs: (33) 1 48 87 58 98
8 Rue des Francs Bourgeois, 75003 Paris
www.entreedesfournisseurs.com

Mokuba: (33) 1 40 13 81 41
18 Rue Montmartre, 75001 Paris
www.mokuba.fr

For craft materials

Rougier & Plé: (33) 1 42 72 82 91 (Paris)
www.crea.tm.fr

Truffaut Ivry: (33) 1 56 20 29 30 (Ivry)
www.truffaut.com

Acknowledgments for photo accessories

The publishers would like to thank the following suppliers for their kind collaboration, and also Truffaut Ivry for the hammock and sunshade.

Addresses

Stanlowa, 250 Rue du Faubourg Saint Honoré, 75008 Paris (33) 145 63 20 96

Muji, 47 Rue des Francs-Bourgeois, 75004 Paris (33) 149 96 41 41

The Conran shop, 117 Rue du Bac, 75007 Paris (33) 142 84 10 01

Entrée des Fournisseurs, 8 Rue des Francs Bourgeois, 75004 Paris (33) 148 87 58 98

Flensted: www.flensted-mobiles.com

Facteur Céleste, 38 Rue Quincampoix, 75004 Paris (33) 142 77 12 46

Moline, 1 Place Saint-Pierre, 75018 (33) 146 06 14 66

Pain d'Epices, 29 Passage Jouffroy, 75009 Paris (33) 147 70 82 65

La Paresse en douce, 97 Rue du Bac, 75007 Paris (33) 142 22 64 10

Moooi: www.moooi.com

C.S.A.O., 1 & 3 Rue Elzevir, 75003 Paris (33) 144 54 55 88

Côté Bastide, 4 Rue de Poissy, 75005 Paris (33) 156 24 01 21

Printemps, 64 Boulevard Haussmann, 75009 Paris (33) 142 82 50 00

Jamin Puech, 68 Rue Vieille du Temple, 75003 Paris (33) 148 87 84 87

Dominique Picquier, 10 Rue Charlot, 75003 Paris (33) 142 72 39 14

Accessories

Moline: trimmings and notions pages 6, 8, 9, 10, 11, 12, 13, 15.

Pain d'Epices: ironing board and irons, page 11.

Entrée des Fournisseurs: ribbons page 15.

La Paresse en Douce: pumps page 44.

The Conran Shop: tableware page 65; milk bottle pages 108, 114–115; red-edged bowl and plate pages 108, 114–115; tray page 209.

Côté Bastide: cup page 108, 113, 115; wh plates, mixing bowl, and jug pages 114–

Printemps: hairbrush and powder com page 136.

Facteur Céleste: dolls pages 180, 182, 18 186; scarf pages 182, 185; clothes pegs pages 185, 186; exercise book page 185

Stanlowa: tutu pages 180, 187, 188, 189; ballet pumps page 189.

Muji: colored pencils page 181.

CSAO: plastic mats pages 208, 209, 210 211, 212.

Moooi: gas candlestick ("Flames"), desig Chris Kabel, page 65.

Jamin Puech: bag page 66.

François Muracciole: designer of radiat page 134.

Flensted: "Futura" mobile FM-110 page

Dominique Picquier: green cushion page

Author's acknowledgments

A warm thank you and many congratulations to the photo design team: Emmanuelle Javelle, Stéphanie Huré; photographs: Marie-Pierre Morel; graphics/layout: Anne Bullat; proofreading: Natacha Kotchetkova and Rose-Marie Di Domenico (my editor) for their ideas, energy, good humor, patience (they certainly needed it!), and enthusiasm.

For their collaboration and support: Lily Alcaraz, Marion Bihel, Elodie Maire, Guy Dupuy, Raphael Dupuy, Mme Dagois, Loulou, Noémie Barré, Camille Soulayrol, Dominique Turbé, Jean-Baptiste Pellerin, Johanna Valeur, Natacha Seret and Arnaud, Renée Méry, Philippe Loheac, M and Mme Sartre, Mme Humilière , Gérard le Mercier, David Page, Fabrice Fix, the TMD studio, Mr "kitchen essentials", Ms "coquette cover-up", and—last but not least—Max.